ANNE WILLAN
FRENCH RECIPES

BOOKS FOR REAL COOKS

PAVILION

Pavilion Books for Real Cooks

Published in Great Britain in 1994 by
PAVILION BOOKS LIMITED
26 Upper Ground, London SE1 9PD

Text © Anne Willan Inc 1994

Recipes originally published by Pavilion in
La France Gastronomique

Design by Write Image
Jacket photograph © Gus Filgate

with thanks to Val Cipollone for editorial assistance

A CIP catalogue record for this book is available from
the British Library

ISBN 1 85793 3982

Printed and bound by WBC Printers, UK

2 4 6 8 10 9 7 5 3 1

This book may be ordered by post direct from the
publisher. Please contact the Marketing Department.
But try your bookshop first.

CONTENTS

FOREWORD

✣

The recipes in this book are the essence of France – a nation which still describes a quarter of its population and much of its landmass as 'profondément rurale'. It is here, in the countryside of France, that the traditions of the kitchen are alive and well.

The surroundings of Château du Feÿ in northern Burgundy, where we live for much of the year, are a case in point. Although only 1 ½ hours from Paris by road, most of our neighbours rarely venture so far. From a hillside overlooking the Yonne river just north of Joigny we command a fine view of the prosperous farmland below, an ever-changing patchwork of crops including roots, grains, and the occasional vineyard. In winter we are sometimes invaded by wild boar from the state forest behind the house.

Our great pride at Le Feÿ is the walled vegetable garden, marked on the property map of 1751. This is the domain of septuagenarian Monsieur Milbert, who plants according to the phases of the moon and despises chemical fertilizer. The sheltered hectare of ground burgeons with fruit, from raspberries, strawberries, plums and a dozen apples and pears, to more esoteric quince, medlar, boysenberries and little wild peaches of incomparable sweetness. Red, white and black currants (the foundation of cassis liqueur) flourish hereabouts, as do black and red cherries, both sweet and tart.

Single-handed, Monsieur Milbert marshals the regimented lines of leeks, onions, garlic and tomatoes, the froth-leaved carrots, bulbous cabbages, bushy green beans, and crawling vines of cucumber and squash. He has even been persuaded to grow sweet corn, though it never reaches his own table. 'Cattlefood!' he growls.

Following tradition, Madame Milbert looks after the poultry yard, raising a flock of chickens and seething hutches of rabbits, each more endearingly fluffy than the last. Her rabbit terrine is a perfect blend of gamey richness. Most nights she simmers a pared down version of 'potée bourguignonne', which traditionally consists of diced shin of beef, a bit of salt pork, a garlic sausage, cabbage heart, potatoes, leeks, celery and turnip. The broth is poured over sliced bread, and the meat and vegetables eaten separately.

In spring Madame Milbert dries lime flowers for herb tea, in summer she sits in the shade of the walnut tree, shelling beans and peas by the hour, while in autumn it is the turn of wild chestnuts, gathered from the avenue outside the gate. Each Christmas we are presented with a bottle of home-brewed cassis liqueur, and of excruciatingly fiery Calvados distilled from Monsieur Milbert's cider.

Good food does not happen by accident; it is the product of the place and the people, of cooks who have had years of practice with an appreciative audience and with ingredients that are just right. It is summed up, I hope, by the 100 recipes in this book. Bon appetit!

Anne Willan
Château du Feÿ
November 1993

SOUPS AND STARTERS
✤

Potage de Potiron

PUMPKIN SOUP

⚜

SERVES 10–12

1 medium–large
pumpkin, about 17 lb/
7.5 kg

1 ⅔ pint/ 1 quart/ 1 litre
milk

2 tbsp butter

1 medium onion,
chopped finely

2 cloves garlic, chopped
finely

2 tbsp flour

1 ⅔ pint/ 1 quart/ 1 litre
chicken stock (p. 150)

1 tbsp curry powder

¼ tsp ground cinnamon

¼ tsp cayenne

salt and pepper

8 fl oz/ 1 cup/ 250 ml
crème fraîche (p. 143) or
double/ heavy cream

8 fl oz/ 1 cup/ 250 ml
double/ heavy cream

8–10 tbsp crème fraîche
(p. 143) or double/
heavy cream (to finish)

8 quart/ 10 quart/ 10 litre
round ovenproof pot

I n 1766, when the novelist Tobias Smollet travelled through Burgundy, he observed 'a vast quantity of very large pompions, with the contents of which [the Burgundians] thicken their soups and ragoûts'.

METHOD

Heat the oven to No 2/ 300°F/ 150°C. Cut a hole in the stem end of the pumpkin, retaining it as a lid. Scoop out the seeds and fibres and discard. Put the pumpkin in an ovenproof pot large enough to contain it. Add the milk to the centre of the pumpkin and replace the lid. Bake it in the heated oven until the flesh is tender, 2–2 ½ hours.

Remove the pumpkin from the oven, take off the lid, and with a large spoon, scrape as much flesh as possible from the hard outer skin. Purée the flesh and milk mixture in a food processor or blender or work it through a sieve. There should be about 4 ⅔ pints/ 3 quarts/ 3 litres of pumpkin purée.

Heat the butter in a large pan, add the onion and garlic, and cook them over low heat until they are transparent but not brown. Stir in the flour and cook for one minute without browning. Whisk in the chicken stock and bring to the boil, stirring constantly until the soup thickens. Add the pumpkin purée, curry powder, cinnamon, cayenne, salt and pepper, and taste the soup for seasoning. Simmer it 5–10 minutes, stirring occasionally.

To finish, bring the soup to the boil, whisk in the crème fraîche and double/ heavy cream, bring just back to the boil and taste for seasoning.

Le Tourin

TOMATO AND GARLIC SOUP

⚜

S ome 'Tourins', vegetable-based soups made with goose fat, need long simmering, but this summer recipe is quick to make with a delightfully fresh flavour. For body, you may like to add a few slivers of 'confit', famed preserved duck of the Périgord, or for a lighter soup the bread croûtes may be replaced by vermicelli, simmered a few minutes in the broth.

METHOD

Heat the fat in a large saucepan and add the onions, garlic, salt and pepper. Press a piece of foil on top and cook gently until the onions are soft, 10–15 minutes. Note: do not let them brown. Stir in the flour, add the tomatoes and leave to cook for 2 minutes. Add the water, bouquet garni, salt and pepper, and simmer, uncovered, 25–30 minutes. Add more water if the soup evaporates too much.

Meanwhile toast the croûtes and put 2–3 in each soup bowl. Taste the soup for seasoning, adding cayenne, salt and pepper, spoon it into bowls and serve very hot.

SERVES 4

3 tbsp goose fat

2 onions, chopped

6 cloves garlic, thinly sliced

salt and pepper

½ oz/ 2 tbsp/ 15 g flour

1 lb/ 500 g tomatoes, peeled, seeded and chopped (p. 151)

16 fl oz/ 1 quart/ 1 litre water, more if needed

bouquet garni (p. 142)

12–18 toasted croûtes (p. 144)

pinch of cayenne

Garbure

GASCON VEGETABLE SOUP

⚜

SERVES 6

3 oz/ 6 tbsp/ 90 g butter

1 medium white turnip, thinly sliced

2 large carrots, thinly sliced

¼ medium head cabbage, shredded

white part of 3 leeks, thinly sliced

2–3 stalks celery, thinly sliced

2 medium potatoes, thinly sliced

2 ⅛ pints/ 1 ½ quarts/ 1.5 litres white veal or chicken stock (p. 150) or water, more if needed

salt and pepper

2–3 long crusty rolls, fried or toasted in croûtes (p. 143)

1 ½ oz/ ½ cup/ 50 g grated Gruyère cheese

2 tbsp chopped parsley

R ecipes for this hearty soup vary from cook to cook and day to day. The best are based on seasonal vegetables from the garden. 'Garbure' may be served unstrained with the vegetables in slivers, or puréed to be quite thick. Croûtes of bread, sometimes topped with the puréed vegetables and grated cheese, then browned in the oven, are the accompaniment. In another variant, the soup is topped with croûtes, then sprinkled with cheese and gratinéed like French onion soup.

METHOD

To cook the dried beans: bring the beans to the boil with enough water to cover by 2 inches/ 5 cm. Cover the pan, remove from the heat, and allow the beans to stand and soften for an hour. Drain the water and put the beans, onion studded with cloves, carrot and bouquet garni in a pan with water to cover. Simmer until the beans are tender, 2–3 hours. Add salt and pepper halfway through the cooking time. Drain the beans, discarding the onion, carrot and bouquet garni.

For the soup: in a large heavy-based saucepan, melt 2 tablespoons of the butter, add the turnip, carrot, cabbage, leek, celery and potato and press a piece of buttered foil on top. Add the lid and cook very gently, stirring occasionally, until the vegetables are fairly tender, about 15–20 minutes. Note: do not let them brown. Add the beans, stock or water, salt and pepper. Cover and simmer until the vegetables are very tender, 20–30 minutes.

Toast or fry the croûtes. Preheat the oven to No 5/ 375°F/ 190°C. Lift out about a quarter of the vegetables from the soup with a slotted spoon and purée them in a food processor or blender. In a small pan, melt a further tablespoon of butter, add the purée and cook, stirring constantly, until it thickens to the consistency of mashed potatoes. Spread the purée on the croûtes, mounding it well, and sprinkle with grated cheese. Bake the croûtes in the heated oven until well browned, 10–12 minutes.

Meanwhile, reheat the soup and add more stock or water if needed to thin it to the consistency of cream. Taste it for seasoning. The soup and croûtes can be made 48 hours ahead and kept covered in the refrigerator.

To finish: bring the soup to the boil and warm the croûtes in the oven. Take the soup from the heat, stir in the remaining butter in small pieces, spoon it into bowls and sprinkle with the chopped parsley. Serve the croûtes separately.

VARIATION

Follow the recipe, but purée all the vegetables together. Just before serving, add the butter and parsley to the soup and pour it into heatproof serving bowls. Cover the surface of each bowl with thin overlapping slices of crusty bread and sprinkle each bowl with 2–3 tablespoons grated Gruyère cheese. Sprinkle on a little melted butter. Bake at No 10/ 500°F/ 260°C until browned, or brown it under the grill/ broiler.

For the dried beans

2 oz/ ⅓ cup/ 60 g dried white haricot beans or navy beans

1 onion studded with 2 cloves

1 small carrot

bouquet garni (p. 142)

salt and pepper

Soupe de Poissons
Languedocienne

LANGUEDOC FISH SOUP

⚜

SERVES 6–8

3 lb/ 1.4 kg mixed fish
with their heads, scaled
and cleaned

1 lb/ 500 g scorpion fish,
or more mixed fish

1 lb/ 500 g conger eel

salt and pepper

2 fl oz/ ¼ cup/ 60 ml
olive oil

3 large onions, sliced

3 cloves garlic, crushed

1 lb/ 500 g tomatoes,
peeled, seeded and
chopped (p. 151)

3 tbsp cognac

large pinch of saffron,
soaked in 3–4 tbsp
boiling water

3 ¼ pints/ 2 quarts/
2 litres water, more if
needed

bouquet garni (p. 142)

2–3 tbsp tomato purée/
paste

cayenne pepper

S corpion fish and conger eel are key ingredients for an authentic 'soupe de poissons', while other possibilities include mullet, bass, bream, and members of the cod family such as hake and whiting. The greater the variety, the better the soup. After sieving, the consistency should be thick and rich but not pulpy. The leftover pounded bones and skin, says one Languedoc cook, 'are the delight of chickens in the farmyard'.

METHOD

Wash and dry the fish and cut them in 1 ½ in/ 4 cm slices, including the heads. Sprinkle them with salt and pepper. In a frying pan, heat half the olive oil and add a layer of fish. Sauté it until lightly browned, about 2 minutes, turn and brown the other side. Remove the fish pieces and sauté the rest in the same way. Heat the remaining oil in the frying pan and fry the onion until soft but not brown, about 5 minutes; remove it.

Pack the fish in a casserole in layers with the onion, garlic, tomato, salt and pepper, setting the slowest cooking fish such as monkfish and conger eel, and the largest pieces, at the bottom. Add the cognac to the frying pan and flame it (p. 145), stirring, to dissolve the pan juices. Pour it over the fish. Add the saffron and liquid, and just enough water to cover the fish. Add the bouquet garni, cover and simmer until the fish flakes very easily, about 1 hour. Meanwhile, prepare the sauce rouille (see below).

Remove the fish and vegetables from the casserole, discarding the bouquet garni, fish heads and as many bones as possible. If necessary, boil the cooking liquid to reduce it until well flavoured. Work the fish and vegetables through a food mill or coarse strainer. Alternatively, purée it in a food processor, taking great care to remove skin and bones beforehand. Whisk the fish purée back into the pot of fish liquid and bring to the boil. Whisk in enough tomato purée/ paste to colour the soup a deep orange. Taste the soup for seasoning, adding cayenne pepper and salt to taste and, if you like, more saffron. The soup and rouille sauce can be refrigerated up to 2 days.

To finish: toast the croûtes. Bring the soup back to the boil; if it is very thick, add more water. Serve it very hot, with separate bowls of croûtes, sauce rouille, and grated cheese. Alternatively, spread the croûtes with rouille and add some to each bowl of soup.

For serving

12 toasted croûtes (p. 144)

3 ¼ oz/ 1 cup/ 100 g grated Gruyère cheese

sauce rouille (see recipe below)

METHOD

If using a dried pepper, soak it in cold water for 20 minutes or until soft enough to remove the seeds. For both fresh and dried pepper, discard stem, core and seeds, then cut it in pieces.

Work the pepper, garlic, egg yolks and a little salt in a food processor until smooth. With the blades running, pour in the olive oil in a thin stream, so the sauce thickens and becomes creamy. Note: if the oil is added too quickly, the mixture will separate. Add tomato purée/ paste for colour if you like. Season the sauce to taste with salt and with cayenne pepper if needed; the flavour should be quite hot.

Sauce Rouille

½ dried or fresh red chilli pepper

4–6 cloves garlic

2 egg yolks

salt

4 fl oz/ ½ cup/ 125 ml olive oil

2–3 tsp tomato purée/ paste (optional)

Pâté de Foie de Pore
Campagnarde

PORK LIVER PÂTÉ

⚜

SERVES 12–15

8 oz/ 250 g sliced
barding fat (p. 141)

1 lb/ 500 g pork liver

1 tbsp butter

1 onion, chopped

1 lb/ 500 g pork (fat and
lean), minced/ ground

8 oz/ 250 g veal,
minced/ ground

2 cloves garlic, finely
chopped

½ tsp ground allspice

pinch ground cloves

pinch ground nutmeg

2 medium eggs, beaten

3 tbsp Calvados

salt and pepper

2 ½ oz/ ½ cup/ 75 g
shelled hazelnuts
(optional)

bay leaf

sprig of thyme

terrine (2 ⅓ pint/
1 ½ quart/ 1.5 litre
capacity)

A splash of Calvados, apply brandy, places this recipe in the Pays de Caux in Normandy. You can use Cognac instead.

METHOD

Line the terrine or casserole with barding fat, reserving a slice for the top. Heat the oven to No 4/ 350°F/ 175°C.

Discard the ducts from the liver and mince/ grind it in a food processor or meat grinder. Melt the butter in a small pan and sauté the onion until soft but not brown. Mix it with the pork, veal, pork liver, garlic, allspice, cloves, nutmeg, eggs, Calvados, and plenty of salt and pepper. Beat with a wooden spoon until the mixture pulls from the sides of the bowl, 2–3 minutes. Sauté a small piece and taste – it should be quite strongly seasoned. Beat in the hazelnuts, if using.

Pack the mixture into the lined terrine and trim the barding fat level with the top. Cut the barding fat in strips and arrange on top of the mixture in a lattice. Set the bay leaf and sprig of thyme on top of the fat. Do not cover the terrine. Set the terrine in a water bath (p. 152), bring it to the boil on top of the stove and transfer to the heated oven. Cook until a skewer inserted in the centre of the terrine for 30 seconds is hot to the touch when withdrawn, 1 ¼–1 ½ hours.

Let the terrine cool until tepid, and then press it with a board or plate with a 2 lb/ 1 kg weight on top until cold. Keep the terrine in the refrigerator for at least 3 days and up to a week to allow the flavour to mellow before serving.

Pâté de Foie de Volaille à l'Ancienne

TRADITIONAL CHICKEN LIVER PÂTÉ

⚜

I t stands to reason that the world's most famous chickens, from Bresse just east of Lyon, make excellent chicken liver pâté. Locally, this pâté is served in an eggcup, just the right size for a single portion.

METHOD

Trim any membrane from the chicken livers and sprinkle them with salt and pepper. In a frying pan heat 2 tablespoons of the butter and fry the livers until thoroughly cooked and crusty brown on the outside, stirring often, 5–7 minutes. Add the shallots and garlic and continue cooking over low heat for 1 minute. Take from the heat, let cool to tepid and work the mixture in a food processor or blender so that it is puréed but there are still bits of the crusty liver to add texture. Cream the remaining butter and beat in the chicken liver purée with the brandy. Season the mixture to taste and spoon into the egg cups or ramekins, smoothing the top. Cover and chill. The pâté can be kept up to 2 days in the refrigerator.

To finish: thin the mayonnaise with a tablespoon or two of warm water so it pours easily. Season the chopped tomato with salt and pepper with salt and pepper and pile it on the pâté. Coat the top with thin mayonnaise and serve at room temperature.

SERVES 8

8 oz/ 250 g chicken livers

salt and pepper

6 oz/ ¾ cup/ 175 g butter

2 shallots, finely chopped

1 clove garlic, crushed

1 tbsp brandy

2 fl oz/ ¼ cup/ 60 ml mayonnaise

1 medium tomato, peeled, seeded and chopped (p. 151)

8 egg cups or ramekins of 2 ½ fl oz/ ⅓ cup/ 75 ml capacity

Terrine de Lapin de Madame Milbert

MADAME MILBERT'S RABBIT TERRINE

⚜

SERVES 10–12

SERVES 10–12

3 lb/ 1.4 kg rabbit, cut in pieces (p. 149), with the liver

1 tbsp butter

2 tbsp brandy

2 tbsp Madeira or sherry

½ tsp ground allspice

pinch of ground cloves

pinch of ground nutmeg

2–3 chicken livers

8 oz/ 250 g thinly sliced barding fat (p. 141)

1 ½ lb/ 750 g belly pork, minced/ ground

1 tbsp salt, or to taste

1 ½ tsp black pepper, or to taste

sprig of thyme

1 bay leaf

3 ¼ pint/ 2 quart/ 2 litre terrine mould

G herkin pickles (cornichons) and black olives are mandatory accompaniments to this game terrine made by our gardener's wife. Chicken can be substituted for the rabbit.

METHOD

With a sharp-pointed knife, cut the meat from the legs of the rabbit, discarding the sinews. Cut the saddle meat from the backbone, and then remove the fillets from under the ribs. Slice the fillets and half the saddle meat lengthwise into long thick strips. Reserve the remaining saddle meat for the stuffing. Heat the butter in a frying pan and cook the strips gently until firm and white, 2–3 minutes. Note: this prevents the meat from shrinking and making hollows in the terrine.

Put the strips in a bowl with the brandy, Madeira or sherry, allspice, cloves and nutmeg, and mix well. Cover and leave to marinate for about an hour. Trim the rabbit and chicken livers of membrane, sprinkle them with salt and pepper and roll them in a sheet of barding fat to form a cylinder as long as the terrine. Line the terrine with the remaining barding fat, reserving a piece for the top.

For the stuffing, work the remaining uncooked rabbit meat, including the meat from the thigh, through the fine blade of a mincer/ grinder with the pork. Drain the marinated strips, and beat the marinade into the pork with the salt and pepper. Fry a small piece of the mixture and taste: it should be highly seasoned.

Heat the oven to No 4/ 350°F/ 175°C. Spread a quarter of the minced/ ground mixture in the lined mould, arrange half the rabbit strips on top, cover with a quarter more mixture, and set the cylinder of livers down the centre. Cover with half the remaining mixture, add the remaining rabbit strips and top with the remaining mixture. Cut the reserved barding fat in strips and arrange in a lattice on top of the meat. Add the thyme and bay leaf.

Set the mould in a water bath (p. 152) and bring to the boil on top of the stove. Cook the terrine, uncovered, in the oven until firm, 1 ½–2 hours. A skewer inserted in the centre should be hot to the touch when withdrawn and the juices should run clear. Let the terrine cool to tepid and then press it overnight with a 2 lb/ 1 kg weight on top. Cover the terrine and refrigerate it for at least two days and up to a week to allow the flavour to mellow. Unmould the terrine for serving, or serve it in the mould, cutting it in thick slices.

Pâté en Croûte Strasbourgeoise
VEAL PÂTÉ IN PASTRY

⚜

SERVES 10–12 AS MAIN
COURSE

12 oz/ 375 g veal
escalope

6 oz/ 175 g pork fat

2 tbsp white wine

2 tbsp brandy

2 tbsp Madeira

salt and pepper

pâte à pâté dough
(p. 148) made with 1 lb/
4 cups/ 500 g flour

8 oz/ 1 cup/ 250 g
unsalted butter, or 3 oz/
6 tbsp/ 90 g lard

5 oz/ ⅔ cup/ 150 g
butter, 2 eggs, 2 tbsp
oil, 2 tsp salt and
2–3 tbsp water

5 oz/ 150 g morel
mushrooms, cleaned
(p. 153)

2 tbsp butter

1 egg, beaten to mix
with ½ tsp salt (for
glaze)

P âté baked in pastry is typical of Strasbourg, the capital of Alsace. This veal pâté, shaped as a freestanding, long loaf, is studded with black morel mushrooms and green pistachios. It can be served warm with Madeira sauce, or baked ahead to serve cold.

METHOD

Cut the veal escalope and pork fat into ¼ inch/ 6 mm strips. Put them in a bowl, add the wine, brandy and Madeira, salt and pepper and mix well. Cover and leave to marinate for 30–45 minutes. Make the pâte à pâté dough and chill 30 minutes. Sauté the mushrooms in the butter with salt and pepper until tender, 3–5 minutes. Butter a baking sheet.

For the stuffing: mix together the veal, pork, ham, pistachios, eggs, nutmeg, allspice, salt and pepper and the marinade drained from the veal. Beat with a wooden spoon or your hand until the stuffing holds together. Cook a piece of the mixture in a frying pan or in the oven, taste, and adjust the seasoning if necessary.

Roll out the dough and trim to a 14 × 20 in/ 35 × 50 cm rectangle. Divide the stuffing into 3 portions. Spread one portion lengthwise on the dough in a 4 × 14 in/ 10 × 35 cm strip. Top with a lengthwise layer of half the strips of marinated veal and half the strips of pork fat, setting half of the morel mushrooms between them. Cover with another portion of stuffing and top with the remaining veal strips, pork fat strips, and mushrooms. Cover with the last portion of stuffing and smooth to make an even layer. Mould the meat with your hands so that the rectangle is compact and tall.

Cut a square of excess dough from each corner and brush the edges of the rectangle with the egg glaze. Lift one long edge of the dough on top of the filling and fold over the opposite edge, pulling tightly to enclose it. Press gently to seal the dough and fold over the ends to make a neat parcel, being sure that the meat is thoroughly enclosed in the dough. Roll the parcel over on to the baking sheet so that the seam is underneath. Brush the pâté with egg glaze.

To decorate the pâté, roll out the dough trimmings, cut a long strip, and set it around the edge of the pâté. Decorate the top with any remaining dough cut in the shapes of leaves or whatever your fancy dictates. Brush the decorations with beaten egg. Make a hole near each end of the pâté and insert a cone of foil as a chimney so that steam can escape. Chill for 30 minutes. Heat the oven to No 6/ 400°F/ 200°C.

Bake the pâté in the heated oven until the pastry is set and starts to brown, about 15 minutes. Turn the heat down to No 4/ 350°F/ 175°C and continue baking until a skewer inserted in the centre of the pâté for half a minute is hot to the touch when withdrawn, about 1 hour. If the pastry browns too much during cooking, cover it loosely with aluminium foil.

For the Madeira sauce, bring the stock to the boil and reduce by one half. Stir in the Madeira and enough dissolved arrowroot to thicken the sauce so it coats the back of a spoon. Taste the sauce for seasoning, adding salt, pepper and more Madeira to taste. The pâté and sauce can be made up to 2 days ahead and refrigerated.

If necessary, reheat the pâté in a moderate (No 4/ 350°F/ 175°C) oven and serve it hot with Madeira sauce. If serving cold, leave the pâté plain and pass gherkin pickles separately.

For the stuffing

1 lb/ 500 g lean veal, minced/ ground

1 ½ lb/ 750 g pork (half fat, half lean) minced/ ground

8 oz/ 250 g lean cooked ham, minced/ ground

4 oz/ ¾ cup/ 125 g pistachios, shelled

2 eggs, beaten to mix

1 tsp ground nutmeg

1 tsp ground allspice

For the Madeira sauce

16 fl oz/ 2 cups/ 500 ml brown stock (p. 149)

3 tbsp Madeira, more if needed

1 tbsp arrowroot, dissolved (p. 141) in 3–4 tbsp water

salt and pepper

Terrine de Legumes à la Mousseline de Veau

VEGETABLE TERRINE WITH VEAL MOUSSELINE

⚜

SERVES 10

1 lb/ 500 g fresh spinach

1 ½ oz/ 3 tbsp/ 45 g unsalted butter

salt and pepper

pinch of grated nutmeg

8 oz/ 250 g carrots, sliced

8 oz/ 250 g turnips, sliced

8 oz/ 250 g green beans, trimmed

For the veal mousseline

1 ½ lb/ 750 g lean veal

1 egg

1 ½ oz/ 3 tbsp/ 45 g unsalted butter, softened

6 fl oz/ ¾ cup/ 175 ml crème fraîche (p. 143) or double/ heavy cream

salt and white pepper

pinch of grated nutmeg

rectangular terrine mould (1 quart/ 1 litre capacity)

A novelty 20 years ago when 'nouvelle cuisine' was launched, vegetable terrine has become a classic. This recipe has more body than most, a mosaic of sliced carrots, turnips, green beans and chopped spinach, all held together with a veal mousseline. The terrine is good served hot with tarragon butter sauce (p. 100) or Montpellier butter (p. 41), or cold with garlic and chilli pepper mayonnaise ('rouille', p. 13).

METHOD

Remove the stems from the spinach and wash thoroughly. Blanch in a pan of boiling salted water for 1 minute. Drain, rinse with cold water and drain again thoroughly, patting it dry with a towel and keeping as many leaves whole as possible. Thoroughly butter the terrine mould and line the bottom and sides with the whole spinach leaves, overlapping the edges of the mould. Chop the remaining leaves. Sauté the chopped spinach in most of the remaining butter until the moisture has evaporated, 2–3 minutes. Season with salt, pepper and nutmeg.

Put the sliced carrots in a pan of cold, salted water, bring to the boil and simmer until tender, 7–10 minutes. Drain thoroughly. Put the turnips in a pan of cold, salted water, bring to the boil and cook until tender, 5–7 minutes. Drain thoroughly. Cook the green beans in a large pan of boiling salted water until just tender, 5–7 minutes. Drain, rinse them in cold water and drain again thoroughly. Sprinkle all the vegetables with salt and pepper. The vegetables can be prepared up to 24 hours ahead and refrigerated.

For the veal mousseline: work the veal in a food processor to a smooth paste. Work in the egg and the softened butter. Set the mixture in a metal bowl over a bowl of ice. Beat until well chilled, then gradually beat in the cream. Season with salt, pepper and nutmeg. Sauté a small piece of mousseline and taste for seasoning.

Heat the oven to No 4/ 350°F/ 175°C. Spread a sixth of the mousseline over the spinach leaves. Arrange the carrot slices on top and cover with more mousseline. Continue adding layers of turnip, mousseline, green beans and spinach, ending with a layer of mousseline. Fold the overlapping spinach leaves on top of the mould. Cover with buttered parchment paper and the lid.

Put the terrine in a water bath and bring to the boil on the stove. Bake in the heated oven until the veal mousseline is set and a skewer inserted in the terrine for 30 seconds comes out hot to the touch, 55–60 minutes. Let stand in a warm place for 10 minutes. If serving hot, turn out the terrine and slice it; serving cold, let it cool completely in the mould.

Soupe au Pistou à la Minute

QUICK VEGETABLE SOUP WITH BASIL AND GARLIC SAUCE

⚜

SERVES 4

2 tbsp butter

2 medium leeks, cut in julienne strips (p. 145), with some of the green

3 stalks celery, cut in julienne strips

2 medium carrots, cut in julienne strips

1 small head lettuce, cut in julienne strips

salt and pepper

1 ⅔ pints/ 1 quart/ 1 litre water

For the pistou

15 basil leaves

3 large cloves garlic, peeled

3 ½ oz/ 1 cup/ 100 g freshly grated Parmesan cheese

4 fl oz/ ½ cup/ 125 ml olive oil

T his version of vegetable soup is so simple that it takes less than half an hour. Essential component is the 'pistou' sauce of garlic, Parmesan cheese, olive oil and basil, the signature herb of Provence.

METHOD

Melt the butter in a large pan. Add the vegetables, seasoning the layers with salt and pepper. Press a piece of buttered wax paper on the vegetables and cover the pan. Cook the vegetables over very low heat until tender, stirring occasionally, 20–25 minutes. Note: do not allow them to brown. Add the water to the vegetables, bring to the boil, then simmer for 5–10 minutes.

Meanwhile make the pistou: chop the basil, garlic and cheese in a food processor or blender, then gradually work in the oil to form a pourable purée. Spoon the soup into bowls and pass the pistou separately. The soup is best freshly made.

Rillettes d'Oie

GOOSE RILLETTES

✤

SERVES 12–16

The finest 'rillettes' consist of pure goose or duck, though they can be stretched by adding pork, preferably from the shoulder, in up to equal quantities. A high proportion of fat is essential and quality is important, as a minimum of seasoning is added so as not to disguise flavour. Pork must be carefully trimmed of sinew so it can be simply pulled apart with two forks after cooking, producing the characteristically soft, rough texture of homemade rillettes.

2 lb/ 1 kg boneless pork shoulder

8–9 lb/ 3.6–4.1 kg whole goose, cut in 8 pieces (p. 144)

⅔ oz/ 1 tbsp/ 20 g salt

⅓ oz/ 1 ½ tsp/ 10 g ground pepper

1 tsp allspice

2 sprigs thyme

2 sprigs rosemary

3 bay leaves

16 fl oz/ 2 cups/ 500 ml water

METHOD

Heat the oven to No ½/ 250°F/ 120°C. Cut the pork in 3 inch/ 7.5 cm cubes. Combine the goose and pork in a heavy pot, layering the pieces with the salt, pepper, allspice, thyme, rosemary and bay leaves and pouring on the water. Mix with your hands and press the meat down lightly. Cover tightly and cook in the oven, stirring occasionally, for 5–6 hours or until the meat is very tender and falling from the bones. The fat should be clear and all the water will have evaporated. Note: cook rillettes very slowly – never let them boil.

Drain the meat, discarding the bay leaves. Reserve the fat and leave it to cool. Shred the meat with two forks, discarding bones and tough goose skin. When the fat is cool, mix half of it with the meat and taste the rillettes. Note: they should be quite highly seasoned. Pack the rillettes into glass jars or stone crocks and pour over enough of the fat to cover. If well sealed with fat, rillettes can be refrigerated for up to 4 weeks. Scrape off excess fat before serving with country bread.

Artichauts à la Barigoule

STUFFED ARTICHOKES WITH BLACK OLIVES

⚜

SERVES 4
—

4 medium globe
artichokes
—

½ lemon
—

1 carrot, sliced
—

1 onion, sliced
—

8 fl oz/ 1 cup/ 250 ml
white wine
—

1 ¼ pints/ 3 cups/
750 ml white veal stock
(p. 150), more if needed
—

salt and pepper
—

1 tbsp arrowroot or
potato flour/ starch,
dissolved (p. 141) in
3 tbsp water
—

S o popular are braised artichokes 'à la barigoule' in southern France that Escoffier, who was born near Nice, included them in his classic *Guide Culinaire*. The name comes from 'farigoule', the local name for thyme. In this recipe, anchovy and olive replace the more classic stuffing based on pork.

METHOD

Preheat the oven to No 4/ 350°F/ 175°C. Break the stem off each artichoke and trim the base so it is flat. Cut off ¾ inch/ 2 cm from the top and trim the spiky tips from the leaves with scissors. Rub the cut surfaces with the lemon half. Parboil the artichokes in boiling salted water for 15–20 minutes and drain them. With a ball cutter or sharp teaspoon, remove the choke and inside leaves.

For the stuffing: melt the butter in a frying pan, add the onion and cook gently until soft but not brown. Add the chopped garlic and the pork and cook over medium heat until crumbling and browned, 5–7 minutes. Stir in the breadcrumbs, mushrooms, ham and olives and leave to cool. Add the basil, parsley, thyme, allspice and pepper and mix thoroughly. Sauté a small piece of stuffing and taste for seasoning; salt may not be needed because the ham and olives are salty.

Fill the hollow of each artichoke with the stuffing and encircle the leaves with string. Put the carrot and onion in a casserole deep enough to contain the artichokes. Add the artichokes with the wine and boil for 5 minutes or until the wine is reduced by half. Pour enough stock over the artichokes to cover them by half, and add salt and pepper. Bring back to the boil, cover with buttered paper, and cook in the oven until tender, 40–50 minutes, basting with the juices occasionally and adding more stock if necessary to keep the artichokes moist. They can be kept in the refrigerator up to a day.

To finish: reheat the artichokes if necessary on top of the stove. Remove them and keep them warm. Strain the cooking liquid into a small saucepan and bring to the boil. Taste the liquid and reduce if necessary until the flavour is concentrated. Whisk in enough of the dissolved arrowroot or potato flour/ starch to obtain a sauce the consistency of thin cream. Simmer for 2 minutes and taste for seasoning. Discard the strings from the artichokes and serve them on individual plates or shallow bowls. Pass the sauce separately.

For the stuffing

1 tbsp butter

½ onion, finely chopped

2 cloves garlic, chopped

4 oz/ 125 g pork, minced/ ground

1 ½ oz/ ½ cup/ 45 g fresh breadcrumbs

2 oz/ 60 g mushrooms, finely chopped

2 oz/ 60 g raw ham, finely diced

2 oz/ 60 g black olives, stoned/ pitted, finely chopped

1 tbsp chopped basil

2 tbsp chopped parsley

1 tsp chopped fresh thyme

large pinch ground allspice

pepper

EGGS AND CHEESE

⚜

Gougères

CHEESE PUFFS

⚜

B urgundians have long been serving this cheese pastry as their traditional accompaniment to a glass of Beaujolais. 'Gougères' should be crisp on the outside but slightly soft in the center.

METHOD

Heat the oven to No 5/ 375°F/ 190°C. Butter a baking sheet. Make the choux pastry (p. 147). Once the pastry has reached the desired consistency, beat in the diced Gruyère.

Transfer the dough to the pastry bag and pipe 2 ½ in/ 6 cm large mounds on the prepared baking sheet. Alternatively, shape the dough with two spoons. Brush the puffs with egg glaze and sprinkle with the grated cheese. Bake in the oven until the gougères are puffed and brown but still slightly soft inside, 30–40 minutes. Gougères are best eaten while still warm, but they can be baked up to 8 hours ahead. Keep them in an airtight container and warm them in a low oven before serving.

Makes 9–10 large gougères

4 oz/ 125 g finely diced Gruyère cheese

1 egg, beaten to mix with ½ tsp salt (for glaze)

1 oz/ 30 g grated Gruyère cheese (for sprinkling)

Pastry bag and ¾ in/ 2 cm plain tube (optional)

Pâte à choux

6 fl oz/ ¾ cup/ 175 ml water

½ tsp salt

2½ oz/ ⅓ cup/ 75 g unsalted butter

4 oz/ 1 cup/ 125 g flour

3–4 eggs

Oeufs en Meurette

POACHED EGGS IN RED WINE SAUCE

⚜

SERVES 4 AS A MAIN COURSE

8 eggs

1 bottle (3 cups/ 750 ml) red burgundy wine

16 fl oz/ 2 cups/ 500 ml brown stock (p. 149)

For the sauce

1 tbsp butter

1 onion, thinly sliced

1 carrot, thinly sliced

1 stick of celery, thinly sliced

1 clove of garlic, crushed

bouquet garni (p. 142)

6 peppercorns

kneaded butter (p. 146) made with 2 tbsp butter and 2 tbsp flour

'Sauce meurette' is a Burgundian classic, a robust mixture of red wine, bacon, mushrooms and baby onions. It is paired with eggs or fish, rivalling any of the more usual sauces with white wine. A fairly light red wine such as a Beaujolais is best for 'meurette' and it must be thoroughly reduced so the sauce is mellow.

METHOD

Poach (p. 145) the eggs, using the wine and stock in place of water and vinegar. Strain the cooking liquid and reserve it.

For the sauce: melt the butter, add the onion, carrot and celery and cook them gently until they are soft but not brown. Add the poaching liquid, garlic, bouquet garni and peppercorns and simmer for 20–25 minutes until the liquid is reduced by half.

Meanwhile, cook the garnish. Melt half the butter in a frying pan and sauté the mushrooms until tender and their moisture has evaporated. Remove them, add the remaining butter and sauté the onions for 10–15 minutes until they are tender and lightly browned, shaking the pan so they colour evenly. Add them to the mushrooms. Finally fry the bacon until it has browned and add it to the mushrooms and onions, discarding the fat from the pan.

To thicken the sauce, first reheat it if necessary and then whisk in the kneaded butter, a piece at a time, until the sauce is thick enough to lightly coat a spoon. Strain it over the garnish and season to taste with salt and pepper. The eggs, sauce and garnish can be kept for up to 2 days in the refrigerator.

To finish: fry the croûtes. Reheat the sauce and garnish on top of the stove if necessary. Reheat the eggs by putting them in hot water for 1 minute, then drain them on paper towels. Set the eggs on the croûtes and put them on a serving dish or on individual plates, allowing two per person. Coat the eggs completely with the sauce.

For the garnish

2 tbsp unsalted butter

3 oz/ 90 g mushrooms, quartered

16–20 baby onions, peeled

3 oz/ 90 g streaky bacon, cut in lardons (p. 146)

salt and pepper

8 round fried croûtes (p. 144), 2 ½ in/ 6 cm in diameter

Oeufs de Pêcheur

FISHERMAN'S EGGS

⚜

**SERVES 8 AS A
STARTER/APPETIZER OR 4
AS A MAIN COURSE**

3 ¼ pints/ 2 quarts/
2 litres mussels

8 fl oz/ 1 cup/ 250 ml dry
white wine, preferably
Muscadet

3 shallots, very finely
chopped

bouquet garni (p. 142)

1 clove garlic, chopped

freshly ground black
pepper

8 eggs

2 tbsp vinegar

2 tbsp potato starch
dissolved (p. 141) in

3–4 tbsp water

2 ½ fl oz/ ⅓ cup/ 75 ml
heavy cream

2 egg yolks

2 tbsp parsley, chopped

8 round fried croûtes
(p. 144)

P oached eggs are perfectly complemented by piquant mussels in a light wine sauce.

METHOD

Clean the mussels (p. 156). In a large saucepan combine the wine, shallots, bouquet garni, garlic and plenty of pepper; bring to the boil and simmer for 2 minutes. Add the mussels, cover and cook over high heat for 5–7 minutes until the mussels open, tossing occasionally. Shell them, discarding any that do not open. Pour the cooking liquid into another saucepan, leaving behind any sand.

Meanwhile, poach the eggs. Bring a large shallow pan of water to the boil. Add the vinegar. Break 4 eggs, one by one, into places where the liquid bubbles. Lower the heat and poach the eggs for 3–4 minutes until the yolk is fairly firm but still soft to the touch. Transfer to a bowl of cold water and trim the stringy edges with scissors. Poach the remaining eggs in the same way.

To finish, reheat the eggs by soaking them in a bowl of hot water for 2 minutes and draining them. Fry the croûtes. Bring the mussel liquid to the boil and whisk in enough of the diluted potato starch to obtain a sauce the consistency of thin cream. Whisk together the cream and egg yolks and stir in about 4 fl oz/ ½ cup/ 125 ml of the hot sauce. Return it to the remaining sauce and cook over low heat, whisking constantly until just slightly thickened. Note: do not boil the sauce or it will curdle. Add the mussels and chopped parsley and heat briefly. Set the eggs on croûtes on individual plates, spooning over the mussels and sauce.

Omelette Gargamelle

OMELETTE WITH MUSHROOMS, CHEESE AND PARSLEY

⚜

G argamelle was one of the carousing characters in the 16th-century *Chronicles of Gargantua* by Rabelais, who spent his childhood in Chinon, on the Loire river. At a local restaurant, you can feast on this puffy 'omelette Gargamelle'.

METHOD

Melt a tablespoon of the butter in a frying pan, add the chopped shallot and cook until soft. Add the mushrooms, salt and pepper. Cook over high heat, stirring occasionally, until their liquid evaporates, 5–10 minutes. Taste the purée for seasoning.

Whisk the eggs with the mushroom purée, salt and pepper until frothy. Stir in the chopped parsley. Heat a further tablespoon of butter in the omelette pan until foaming and add half the eggs. Cook, stirring constantly with a fork, until lightly set and brown on the bottom. Spread half the cream cheese in the centre, leave it to warm for 30 seconds and then fold the omelette, tipping it into an oval baking dish. Repeat with the second omelette.

For the cream sauce: scald the milk. Melt the butter in a heavy saucepan, whisk in the flour and cook until foaming, about 1 minute. Remove the pan from the heat and strain in the hot milk, whisking constantly. Bring the sauce back to the boil, whisking constantly, until it thickens. Add the crème fraîche, season to taste with salt, pepper and nutmeg and simmer for 2 minutes. Pour it over the omelettes and sprinkle with the grated cheese.

To finish: heat the oven to No 6/ 400°F/ 200°C. Bake the omelettes until the cheese is melted and the sauce bubbling, about 5 minutes. Serve at once.

SERVES 2

3 tbsp butter

1 shallot, chopped

4 oz/ 125 g mushrooms, finely chopped

salt and pepper

5 eggs

2 tbsp chopped parsley

2 oz/ ¼ cup/ 60 g soft cream cheese

1 tbsp grated Gruyère cheese (for sprinkling)

For the cream sauce

8 fl oz/ 1 cup/ 250 ml milk

1 tbsp butter

1 tbsp flour

2 fl oz/ ¼ cup/ 60 ml crème fraîche (p. 143) or heavy/ double cream

salt and white pepper

a pinch of nutmeg

8 in/ 20 cm omelette pan; 2 small baking dishes

Omelette de la Garrigue

SNAIL, HAM AND WALNUT OMELETTE

❧

SERVES 2

2 oz/ ½ cup/
60 g canned snails,
drained and rinsed

1 ½ oz/ 3 tbsp/
45 g unsalted butter

1 oz/ ⅓ cup/
30 g country ham, finely
diced

1 clove garlic, chopped

salt and pepper

3 tbsp coarsely chopped
walnuts

2 tbsp chopped parsley

5 eggs

9–10 in/ 22–25 cm
omelette pan

 amed for the herb-scented scrub on which the snails feed, this omelette is a speciality of the Languedoc and robust with flavour.

METHOD

Cut each snail in 2–3 pieces. Melt half the butter in a frying pan, add the snails, ham, garlic, salt and pepper and cook them gently for 4–5 minutes. Take the pan from the heat and stir in the walnuts and parsley.

To cook the omelette: whisk the eggs with a pinch of salt and pepper until they are well mixed. If necessary, warm the snail mixture over a low heat. Heat the remaining butter in the omelette pan, add the eggs and stir briskly with a fork, pulling the cooked eggs from the sides to the centre of the pan. After 10 seconds, stir in the snail mixture and continue cooking for 5–10 seconds longer until the mixture is almost as thick as scrambled eggs. Leave the omelette on the heat until browned on the bottom and still soft on top if you like a soft omelette, or almost firm if you like it well done.

Fold the omelette, tipping the pan away from you and turning the edge with a fork. Half roll, half slide the omelette on to a warm serving dish so it lands folded in three. Serve at once.

Fromage Fort

PIQUANT SOFT CHEESE

⚜

'F romage fort' is sometimes called 'claqueret' from the verb 'claquer', to slap, an action which keeps wives and cheese in order, say the Lyonnais. Serve fromage fort with hot boiled or steamed potatoes or as a spread for bread or toast. Alternatively it can be thinned with cream and served as a dressing for potato or cucumber salad.

METHOD

Put the leeks in a saucepan with the thyme and tarragon and add water to barely cover them. Bring to the boil and simmer for 20 minutes. Drain the liquid through a fine sieve, pressing hard on the vegetables to extract all the juices. Let it cool completely and measure the liquid, adding more water if necessary to make 4 fl oz/ ½ cup/ 125 ml.

Beat the cheese until very smooth. Whisk in the vegetable liquid, cream, marc or brandy, oil and vinegar. Stir in the garlic and chives with salt and plenty of pepper to taste. Spoon the mixture into a small bowl or crock. The flavour mellows if it is kept at least 3 days and up to 2 weeks.

SERVES 6–8

1 large or 2–3 small leeks, washed, trimmed and sliced

1 sprig thyme

1 tbsp tarragon leaves

1 lb/ 500 g fresh goat or cows' cream cheese

2 ½ fl oz/ ⅓ cup/ 75 ml double/ heavy cream or crème fraîche (p. 143)

2 tbsp marc or brandy

1 tbsp oil

1 tbsp wine vinegar

3 cloves garlic, finely chopped

3 tbsp chopped chives

salt and pepper

boiled or steamed potatoes, fresh bread or toast (for serving)

Tarte au Fromage de Chèvre et sa Salade de Chou Vert aux Noix

FRESH GOAT CHEESE QUICHE, CABBAGE AND WALNUT SALAD

⚜

SERVES 6

1 small Savoy cabbage (about 1 ½ lb/ 750 g)

8 oz/ 250 g fresh goat cheese

10 in/ 25 cm tart tin/ pan

Pâte brisée

6 ½ oz/ 1 ⅔ cups/ 200 g flour

3 ¼ oz/ 7 tbsp/ 100 g butter

1 egg yolk

½ tsp salt

3–5 tbsp cold water

For the white sauce

12 fl oz/ 1 ½ cups/ 375 ml milk

3 tbsp butter

3 tbsp flour

6 fl oz/ ¾ cup/ 175 ml crème fraîche (p. 143) or double/ heavy cream

salt and pepper

oat cheeses of all kinds, from fresh to tart and well-aged, are a speciality of the Loire. In this recipe, shredded cabbage and crumbled soft goat cheese are baked in a custard filling, while more cabbage is tossed with walnuts in a walnut oil dressing to serve with the finished tart. Walnut groves have largely disappeared from the region, but a taste for the nut remains.

METHOD

Make the pâte brisée (p. 147) and chill it for 30 minutes. Roll out the dough and line the tart tin/ pan. Blind bake the shell (p. 141).

Trim the outer leaves from the cabbage and finely shred it, discarding the core. Boil a large pan of salted water, add the cabbage and bring just back to the boil. Drain, rinse with cold water and drain thoroughly.

For the white sauce: scald the milk. Melt the butter in a heavy saucepan, whisk in the flour and cook until foaming, about 1 minute. Remove the pan from the heat and strain in the hot milk, whisking constantly. Bring the sauce back to the boil, whisking constantly, until it thickens. Note: it will be very thick. Add the crème fraîche, season to taste with salt, pepper and nutmeg and simmer for 2 minutes. Let the sauce cool to lukewarm.

Heat the oven to No 5/ 375°F/ 190°C. Spread about a third of the cabbage in the pie shell. Crumble the goat cheese on top. Stir the egg and egg yolks into the sauce and season again to taste. Pour the mixture into the pie shell.

Bake the quiche in the heated oven until brown

and firm, 40–45 minutes. A skewer inserted in the centre should come out clean. Let the quiche cool, then unmould it and serve at room temperature. It is best eaten the day of baking.

For the salad: make the vinaigrette (p. 152). About 30 minutes before serving, toss the remaining cabbage with the walnuts and dressing and serve with the quiche.

pinch of grated nutmeg

1 egg

2 egg yolks

For the vinaigrette dressing

2 fl oz/ ¼ cup/ 60 ml red wine vinegar

salt and pepper

1 tsp Dijon mustard

2 fl oz/ ¼ cup/ 60 ml walnut oil

2 fl oz/ ¼ cup/ 60 ml salad oil

3–4 tbsp coarsely chopped walnuts

FISH AND SHELLFISH

⚜

Dos de Saumon Lardé au Raifort

SADDLE OF SALMON WITH BACON AND HORSERADISH CREAM

❧

S almon was once plentiful in the Rhine, often combined on Alsatian menus with Germanic flavourings like horseradish.

METHOD

Put the lentils in a saucepan with the onion, garlic, bouquet garni, some pepper, and enough water to cover generously. Cover and simmer for 30 minutes, stirring occasionally. Add salt with more water if the lentils seem dry, and continue simmering until they are tender, 20–30 minutes longer. The lentils should be soupy, but most of the water should be absorbed. Discard the onion, bouquet garni and garlic and taste for seasoning.

To cook the salmon, heat the oven to No 3/ 325°F/ 160°C. With the point of a knife, poke holes in both sides of the salmon and insert a lardon of bacon in each one. Spread the salmon with butter, sprinkle it with pepper and set it in a flame-proof baking dish. Bake it in the heated oven, basting often until a skewer inserted in the centre is hot to the touch when withdrawn after half a minute, 30–40 minutes.

To finish, reheat the lentils if necessary on top of the stove. Transfer the salmon to a serving platter, cover loosely with foil and keep it warm. Discard the fat from the baking dish, add the cream and bring it to the boil, stirring to dissolve the pan juices. Strain the cream into a separate pan, add the horseradish and shallots with salt and pepper to taste, bring back to the boil and simmer for 2 minutes. Spoon the lentils around the salmon and serve the sauce separately.

SERVES 8 AS A MAIN COURSE

2 lb/ 1 kg piece of centre cut salmon on the bone, scales removed

4 oz/ 125 g piece of bacon, cut in thin lardons (p. 146)

1 ½ oz/ 3 tbsp/ 45 g butter

salt and pepper

12 fl oz/ 1 ½ cups/ 375 ml crème fraîche (p. 143) or double/ heavy cream

2 tbsp grated fresh horseradish, or 3–4 tbsp bottled horseradish

2 shallots, finely chopped

For the lentils

8 oz/ 250 g lentils

1 onion, studded with a clove

1 clove garlic

bouquet garni (p. 142)

16 fl oz/ 2 cups/ 500 ml water, more if needed

Truite au Jambon de Bayonne

SAUTÉED TROUT WITH BAYONNE HAM

⚜

SERVES 4

4 trout each weighing
about 8 oz/ 250 g

salt and pepper

1 oz/ ¼ cup/ 30 g flour

2 oz/ ¼ cup/ 60 g butter

2 shallots, chopped

2 cloves garlic, chopped

2 oz/ ¼ cup/ 60 g
Bayonne, prosciutto, or
other raw smoked ham,
diced

2 tbsp wine vinegar

2 tbsp chopped parsley

I t was years ago in a little mountain restaurant that I first tasted trout with the piquant smoked ham of Gascony, and I've enjoyed it ever since. Prosciutto or any other raw smoked ham may be substituted.

METHOD

Cut the fins off the trout and trim the tails to a 'V'. If they are not already cleaned, clean them through the gills without slitting the stomach. Wash the fish thoroughly and pat dry. Sprinkle the trout with salt and pepper and coat with flour, patting off the excess.

Heat the butter in a large frying pan, add the trout and sauté them until golden brown and they just flake easily, 4–5 minutes on each side. Transfer them to a platter, cover and keep warm.

Add the shallot to the hot pan and sauté briefly until soft. Stir in the garlic and ham and cook 1 minute. Remove the pan from the heat, add the vinegar, and then the parsley, standing back as it will splutter. While still foaming, pour the vinegar and ham mixture over the fish and serve immediately.

Escargots sur un Champ Rouge et Vert

SNAILS ON A FIELD OF TOMATO AND PARSLEY

⚜

The finest snails, say connoisseurs, are fattened on a diet of lettuce and herbs such as thyme. The snails for this recipe may be canned or frozen and their shells are not needed as the snails are set on a bed of tomato coulis and parsley purée.

METHOD

To make the tomato coulis: melt the butter in a saucepan and add the tomatoes, bouquet garni, salt and pepper. Simmer, uncovered, until the tomatoes are very soft and thick, 15–20 minutes. Discard the bouquet garni and taste for seasoning.

To make the parsley purée: discard the parsley stems. Blanch (p. 141) the sprigs, drain, rinse them with cold water and drain thoroughly. Purée the parsley in a food processor or blender with the cream and season to taste with salt and pepper. Tomato coulis and parsley purée can be stored up to 24 hours in the refrigerator.

To finish: warm the tomato coulis and parsley purée over low heat, adding a little water to the purée if necessary so it spreads easily. Heat the butter in a frying pan and sauté the snails for 2 minutes. Add the garlic, shallot, salt and pepper and continue cooking for 1–2 minutes until the snails are very hot. Spoon the tomato coulis on one side of 4 warm individual plates, then add the parsley on the other. Pile the snails in the centre and serve at once.

SERVES 4

2 oz/ ¼ cup/ 60 g butter

24 large or 36 small cooked snails

1–2 cloves garlic, finely chopped

1 shallot, finely chopped

salt and pepper

For the tomato coulis

1 tbsp butter

2 lb/ 1 kg tomatoes, peeled, seeded and chopped (p. 151)

bouquet garni (p. 142)

For the parsley purée

2 bunches of parsley (about 4 oz/ 125 g)

4 fl oz/ ½ cup/ 125 ml double/ heavy cream

Baudroie Rôtie au Beurre de
Montpellier

GRILLED BROILED MONKFISH WITH PIQUANT HERB BUTTER

⚜

a 4 ½ lb/ 2 kg monkfish
(or two 2 lb/ 1 kg
monkfish)

2 tbsp olive oil

2–3 sprigs thyme

2–3 sprigs oregano or
marjoram

salt and pepper

lettuce leaves (for
garnish)

Montpellier butter (for
serving – see recipe
opposite)

T he herb butter on this fish is a classic of the Languedoc but a new-style chef would be justly proud of its lightness. 'Baudroie' is the local name for monkfish.

METHOD

Skin the monkfish, also cutting away the membrane under the skin. Cut horizontally along one side of the central bone towards the backbone to remove the fillet. Repeat on the other side to remove the second fillet. Brush the olive oil over the fish, add the herbs and sprinkle with salt and pepper. It may be prepared up to 2 hours ahead; cover and keep in the refrigerator. Meanwhile, prepare the Montpellier butter.

Preheat the grill-broiler. Put the monkfish fillets on a baking sheet lined with foil and baste again with the oil and herbs. Set the pan 3 ins/ 7.5 cm from the heat and grill/ broil the fillets until lightly browned, about 10 minutes for small fish or 15 minutes for a larger one, basting occasionally with oil and herbs. Turn them and grill/ broil the other side until brown and the fish is no longer transparent in the centre when tested with a fork, 5–7 minutes.

Arrange the lettuce leaves on a serving platter and set the fish on top. Serve the Montpellier butter separately in a sauceboat.

MONTPELLIER BUTTER

Discard the stems from the watercress and spinach and the large stalks from the parsley and chervil. Blanch (p. 141) the leaves, drain them, then squeeze them dry in a cloth.

Drain the anchovies and work them in a food processor with the pickle, capers and garlic until finely chopped. Add the butter gradually, continuing to purée until smooth. Add the herbs and purée until finely chopped. With the blades turning, slowly pour in the olive oil. Add the mustard and season with lemon juice, salt and pepper to taste.

If not using a food processor, finely chop the blanched herbs, anchovies, pickles, capers and garlic together with a knife. Cream the butter, beat in the herb mixture and mustard until smooth and then gradually beat in the oil. Season the sauce with lemon juice, salt and pepper to taste.

Montpellier Butter

a medium bunch (½ oz/ 15 g) watercress

a medium handful (½ oz/ 15 g) spinach leaves

a medium bunch (½ oz/ 15 g) parsley sprigs

a medium bunch (½ oz/ 15 g) fresh chervil

2 anchovy fillets, soaked in water or milk

1 small gherkin pickle

2 tsp capers, drained

½ clove garlic, peeled

2 ½ oz/ ⅓ cup/ 75 g butter, softened

3 tbsp olive oil

1 tsp Dijon mustard

a few drops lemon juice

salt and pepper

Brandade de Morue aux Olives Vertes

PURÉE OF SALT COD WITH GREEN OLIVES

⚜

SERVES 6–8

1 ½ lb/ 750 g salt cod

1 lb/ 500 g potatoes, peeled

8 fl oz/ 1 cup/ 250 ml olive oil

8 fl oz/ 1 cup/ 250 ml milk

1 ½ oz/ ⅓ cup/ 45 g green olives, stoned/ pitted

1 clove garlic (optional)

12 triangular fried croûtes (p. 144) rubbed with a halved garlic clove

pinch of grated nutmeg

a few drops of lemon juice

white pepper

salt (optional)

'Brandade' is a purée of salt cod, potatoes, olive oil and hot milk, all beaten together to fluffy lightness. It can be made by hand, but the food processor will greatly lighten the work. Traditionally, the purée is served with fried garlic croûtons and a jet-black garnish of ripe olives, but here fresher-tasting green olives are added to the purée. At its best piping hot, with the cod thoroughly blanched of its salt and flavoured with fruity olive oil, 'brandade' is a speciality of Nîmes.

METHOD

Soak the cod in cold water for 1–2 days, changing the water several times. Drain it, put it in a large pan of cold water, cover and bring just to the boil. Poach over a low fire for 8–10 minutes or until barely tender, drain and cool it slightly. Flake the flesh with a fork, discarding all skin and bone.

Cook the potatoes by simmering them in lightly salted water until tender, 15–20 minutes. Drain them, return them to a low fire for a few seconds to dry, then cut them into small pieces.

Heat two-thirds of the oil in a saucepan until very hot. Scald the milk in another saucepan. Put the flaked cod in a food processor and with the blades turning, slowly pour in the hot oil. Add the olives and the garlic, if using, and purée thoroughly. Then add the remaining oil, little by little, alternating with the hot milk. Finally, add the potato pieces a few at a time to the cod mixture with the blades running; purée just until smooth.

If not using a food processor, heat two-thirds of the oil in a saucepan until very hot; scald the milk in another saucepan. Add the flaked cod to the oil and beat vigorously with a wooden spoon over a low fire, crushing and separating the fibres; to prevent the cod from browning move the pan on and off the fire as you beat. Finely chop the garlic and olives and stir them in. Beat in a tablespoon of the milk. Work the potato through a fine sieve, or purée it with a potato masher. Beat it into the cod purée.

Fry the croûtes. Season the brandade to taste with grated nutmeg, lemon juice and pepper; salt may not be needed as the cod is salty. The finished purée should be white, smooth and stiff enough to hold its shape. If it is very stiff, beat in a little more milk. Pile the brandade in a shallow bowl, surround it with the croûtes, and serve at once.

Tielles de Sète

PIES WITH MUSSELS, SQUID AND ANCHOVY

⚜

Makes 6 pies

8 oz/ 250 g squid

2 lb/ 1 kg mussels, cleaned (p. 156)

4 anchovy fillets

2 cloves garlic, finely chopped

3 tbsp chopped mixed herbs – parsley, thyme, oregano

pepper

1 egg, beaten to mix with ½ tsp salt (for glaze)

six 4 in/ 10 cm tartlet tins/ pans: fluted pastry cutters 5 in/ 12.5 cm and 4 in/ 10 cm diameter

Pâte brisée

1 lb/ 4 cups/ 500 g flour

8 oz/ 1 cup/ 250 g unsalted butter, or 1 part lard, 2 parts unsalted butter

1 egg

1 ½ tsp salt

8–10 tbsp cold water

A speciality of Sète in the Languedoc, 'tielles' are pungent and robust. You'll find a spoonful of Montpellier butter (p. 41) (if the pies are hot) or 'aïoli', garlic mayonnaise (if cold) does not come amiss.

METHOD

Make the pâte brisée dough (p. 147) and chill 30 minutes. Meanwhile clean the squid: pull the body from the head and, if the ink sac is unbroken, pierce it and catch the ink in a small bowl. Open the tentacles to reveal the 'beak' in the centre. Squeeze it outwards, cut off and discard it. Cut the tentacles from the head and intestines; discard the head and intestines also. Cut the tentacles into slices and the body into rings.

Put the cleaned mussels in a large saucepan, cover and cook over high heat, stirring once, until the mussels open, 4–5 minutes. Discard any mussels that do not open. Lift out the mussels and take the meat from the shells, discarding the rubbery ring. Pour the mussel liquid into a small saucepan, leaving sand and grit behind. Add the squid with enough water to cover. Simmer the squid until tender, 2–3 minutes.

For the stuffing: chop the mussels, squid and anchovy in a food processor or by hand with a knife. Stir in the squid ink (if the ink sac was unbroken), garlic, herbs and plenty of pepper. Taste, adding salt only if necessary. The stuffing should be highly flavoured.

Roll out the pastry dough to ⅛ in/ 3 mm thickness and stamp out 8 rounds with each pastry cutter. Line the tartlet tins/ pans with the larger rounds of dough, overlapping the edges over the tins/ pans. Brush the edges with egg glaze. Spread the stuffing inside and top with the smaller rounds. Press the dough edges together then decorate them, folding the double layer with your finger and thumb alternately inwards and outwards so the edge of the pies is fluted. Cut a hole in the pies for steam to escape, brush them with egg glaze and chill 15 minutes. Preheat the oven to No 6/ 400°F/ 200°C.

Set the pies in the lower half of the heated oven and bake until crisp and brown underneath as well as on top, 25–30 minutes. They are best eaten the day of baking, but can be refrigerated 2 days and warmed just before serving.

Coquilles Saint-Jacques au Safron

SCALLOPS WITH SAFFRON

SERVES 4–6

2 tbsp butter

6 oz/ 175 g mushrooms, thinly sliced

juice of ½ lemon

salt and pepper

2 lb/ 1 kg shelled sea scallops

large pinch of saffron threads, soaked in 2–3 tbsp boiling water

For the sauce

1 shallot, finely chopped

2 tbsp dry vermouth

2 tbsp white wine

½ pint/ 1 ¼ cups/ 300 ml crème fraîche (p. 143) or double/ heavy cream

small pinch saffron threads, optional

3 oz/ 6 tbsp/ 90 g cold butter

T he combination of saffron with scallops is hard to beat for harmony of flavour. Rice pilaf is a good foil for the rich sauce.

METHOD

Melt half the butter in a medium pan and add the mushrooms, lemon juice, salt and pepper and press a piece of buttered foil on top. Cover with the lid and cook gently until the mushrooms are tender, 4–5 minutes.

Melt the remaining butter in a frying pan, add the scallops and pour over the saffron and liquid. Cover and cook very gently until the scallops whiten, 3–5 minutes. Note: do not overcook them or they will be tough. Transfer them to a plate with a draining spoon.

For the sauce: add any cooking juices from the mushrooms to the scallop liquid with the shallot, vermouth and wine. Boil until reduced to a glaze (p. 145). Whisk in the cream, and boil until reduced by about a third, 5–7 minutes. Taste, adding more saffron if necessary. Scallops and sauce can be cooked up to 2 hours ahead.

To finish: reheat the sauce if necessary. Take the pan from the heat and whisk in the cold butter, working on and off the heat so that it softens without melting to oil. When all the butter is added, bring the sauce just to the boil. Add the scallops and mushrooms, heat gently for 1–2 minutes and spoon the mixture on to individual warm plates.

Sole Sautée Joinville

SAUTÉED SOLE WITH SHRIMPS AND MUSHROOMS

⚜

D over sole is the preferred fish for sautéing, but any white fish fillets can be substituted. This dish with shrimp and mushrooms is named after the Norman town of Joinville.

METHOD

Wash the sole fillets and dry them on paper towels. Dip them in seasoned flour, patting them to coat evenly.

In a heavy frying pan or skillet, heat half the butter until foaming, add the fillets, skinned (smooth) side down. (If all the fillets won't fit, fry them in two batches.) Fry over brisk heat until golden brown, 1–2 minutes, depending on the thickness of the fish; turn over and brown the other side.

Note: the fish will flake in pieces if overcooked. Transfer the fillets to a serving dish and keep warm.

Wipe out the pan and heat the remaining butter until foaming. Add the shrimps and heat, stirring for 30 seconds; remove them. Add the mushrooms and sauté until all the cooking liquid has evaporated, 5–7 minutes.

Stir the shrimps into the mushrooms with the lemon juice, salt and pepper, and taste. Spoon the mixture over the fish, sprinkle with parsley and serve at once.

SERVES 8 AS AN APPETIZER AND 4 AS A MAIN COURSE

8 sole fillets, about 1 ½ lb/ 750 g

2 oz/ ½ cup/ 60 g flour seasoned with ½ teaspoon salt and pinch of white pepper

5 oz/ ⅔ cup/ 150 g butter

4 oz/ 125 g cooked, peeled, baby shrimps

8 oz/ 250 g mushrooms, thinly sliced

juice of 1 lemon

2 tbsp chopped parsley

Marmite Dieppoise

FISH STEW WITH VEGETABLES AND CREAM

⚜

fillets of 4 lemon sole,
flounder or whiting
weighing about 1 lb/
500 g each

8 cod steaks, weighing
1 ½ lb/ 750 g

1 ⅔ pint/ 1 quart/ 1 litre
fish stock (p. 150)

2 ½ oz/ ⅓ cup/ 75 g
butter

2 leeks, trimmed, split
and chopped

2 large onions, chopped

1 tsp curry powder, or to
taste

pinch of paprika

2 tomatoes, peeled,
seeded and chopped
(p. 151)

4 medium carrots,
peeled and cut in sticks

4 stalks celery, cut in
sticks

8 fl oz/ 1 cup/ 250 ml
white wine

salt and pepper

T he use of spice in this Dieppoise fish stew
dates from medieval times when Dieppe, on
the coast of Normandy, was an important trading
port. 'Marmite Dieppoise' is a good deal more
serious than the usual fisherman's stew of his leftover catch. A good marmite includes mussels,
shrimps, scallops and a scampi or two. In the old
days, you might have found Dover sole and turbot
among the white fish, but nowadays it is more
likely to be lemon sole or whiting.

METHOD

Cut each fillet in half crosswise. Cut each cod
steak in 4 pieces, removing the bone. Use the
heads, tails and bones of the fish to make a simple
stock: wash them, put them in a large pan and
add enough water to cover, bring to the boil and
simmer for 20 minutes. Strain; then add enough
water to make 1 ⅔ pints/ 1 quart/ 1 litre liquid.
Wash the pieces of fish and pat them dry.

Heat 2 tablespoons of the butter in a saucepan.
Add the chopped leeks and onions and cook over
low heat, stirring occasionally, until soft but not
brown. Stir in the curry powder and paprika and
cook for 1 minute. Add the tomatoes, carrots,
celery, wine and fish stock with a little salt and
pepper and simmer until the vegetables are almost
tender, about 15 minutes.

Meanwhile layer the fish in a large saucepan,
first the cod, then the scallops, sole, flounder or
whiting, and mussels, sprinkling each layer with salt
and pepper. Pour over the vegetable broth, bring
to the boil and simmer until the fish just flakes

easily and the mussels open, 3–5 minutes. Discard any mussels that do not open when heated.

Transfer the fish and mussels to serving bowls. Add cream and cayenne to the broth, bring to the boil and taste – it should be slightly piquant with cayenne. Add the shrimps and spoon them with the vegetables and broth over the fish. Serve at once.

8 scallops

3 ½ pints/ 2 quarts/ 2 litres mussels, cleaned (p. 146)

8 fl oz/ 1 cup/ 250 ml crème fraîche (p. 143) or double/ heavy cream

pinch of cayenne pepper

8 oz/ 250 g cooked peeled shrimps

Saumon et Celeris à l'Huile de Noix

SALMON WITH CELERY AND WALNUT OIL

⚜

SERVES 4

1 ¼ lb/ 625 g salmon fillet, or 4 salmon steaks

2 cloves garlic, finely chopped

4 tbsp chopped, mixed herbs (chives, chervil, tarragon, parsley)

2 tbsp white wine

4 fl oz/ ½ cup/ 125 ml walnut oil

salt and pepper

small head celery (about 12 oz/ 375 g) trimmed and cut in julienne strips (p. 145)

3 tbsp double/ heavy cream

2 oz/ ¼ cup/ 60 g cold butter, cut in pieces

1 tsp lemon juice, or to taste

T his contemporary recipe calls for salmon, depicted in prehistoric cave paintings and now reappearing in the Périgord's Dordogne river, thanks to conservation efforts. Cold-pressed walnut oil is one of the treats of the region.

METHOD

If using salmon fillet, cut it into 4 even diagonal slices about ½ in/ 1.25 cm thick ('escalopes'); if using steaks, leave them whole. In a shallow dish, mix the garlic, herbs, wine, half of the oil, the salt and pepper. Lay the salmon escalopes on top, turning them so they are well coated. Cover and leave to marinate at room temperature ½–1 hour. Preheat the oven to No 10/ 500°F/ 260°C. Blanch (p. 141) the celery, drain and rinse in cold water.

Lightly oil a baking dish, lay the celery on top and sprinkle with salt and pepper. Top with the salmon escalopes or steaks (they should not overlap). Bake them in the oven until the salmon no longer looks transparent, 6–8 minutes. Note: the salmon should remain slightly transparent in the centre as it will continue cooking in its own heat. Arrange the fish and celery on individual serving plates, and keep warm.

Meanwhile, put the marinade in a small saucepan; add the cream and boil until reduced to a glaze (p. 145), 2–3 minutes. Whisk in the butter a few pieces at a time, working on and off the heat so it softens creamily without melting to oil. Take the pan from the heat and whisk in the remaining oil in a slow, steady stream. Add the lemon juice, taste for seasoning and spoon around the fish.

Poisson au Four Chef Guy

BAKED FISH WITH TOMATO, POTATO AND GARLIC

⚜

lmost any well-flavoured fish can be used here. Breton Chef Guy Diqueliou is particularly fond of sea bass and salmon trout. He leaves the scales on the fish to retain moisture, so it should be skinned before serving.

METHOD

In a frying pan heat 2 tablespoons of the olive oil and sauté the onions until soft but not brown. Oil a large baking dish and spread in it the tomatoes, sautéed onions, shallots, garlic, and finally the potatoes. Season with salt and pepper. The vegetables should form a bed about 1 in/ 2.5 cm thick.

Wash the fish, trimming the tail and fins but leaving the head intact. Score the flesh deeply with 3 or 4 slashes on each side so that it cooks evenly. Set the fish on top of the vegetables in the gratin dish and tuck a sprig of fresh thyme into each of the slashes. Spoon the rest of the oil over the fish and sprinkle with salt, pepper, the juice of the lemon and the white wine. The fish can be prepared up to 3 hours ahead and kept in the refrigerator.

Heat the oven to No 3/ 325°F/ 160°C. Bake the fish uncovered, basting occasionally, until it just flakes easily, about ¾–1 hour for the larger fish and 30–45 minutes for the smaller fish.

If the vegetables are not tender, remove the fish, wrap it in foil and keep warm. Turn the oven heat to No 6/ 400°F/ 200°C and continue baking the vegetables until cooked and brown on top.

To serve, discard the foil, set the fish on the vegetables, add a garnish of lemon wedges and serve.

SERVES 4–6

6–8 tbsp olive oil

4 medium onions, thinly sliced

1 ½ lb/ 750 g tomatoes, peeled, seeded and chopped

4 shallots, thinly sliced

6 cloves garlic, thinly sliced

2 lb/ 1 kg potatoes, peeled and thinly sliced

salt and pepper

one 4 ½ lb/ 2 kg whole fish, or two 3 lb/ 1.25 kg fish, cleaned but not scaled

6–8 sprigs fresh thyme

juice of 1 lemon

4 fl oz/ ½ cup/ 125 ml white wine

1 lemon, cut in wedges (for garnish)

Ballotine de Brochet
Rabelaisienne

BALLOTINE OF PIKE AND SALMON TROUT
WITH PRUNES, RED BUTTER SAUCE

⚜

SERVES 12

24 prunes

1 bottle (750 ml) Chinon
or other fruity red wine

2 pike fillets
(1 ¼ – 1 ½ lb/
600-750 g), skinned

For the sauce

8 oz/ 1 cup/ 250 g chilled
unsalted butter, cut into
pieces

2 onions, sliced

2 stalks celery, sliced

2 carrots, sliced

bouquet garni (p. 142)

4 cloves garlic

1 lb/ 500 g fish bones

4 shallots, chopped

2 ½ fl oz/ ⅓ cup/ 75 ml
red wine vinegar

1 tsp tomato purée/
paste

2 tbsp double/ heavy
cream

E ven though fish is now scarce in the Loire, a tradition of fish recipes continues in the region. This pâté of pink salmon trout mousse is sandwiched between fillets of pike and studded with prunes, another local ingredient. Indeed, plums are so common that a local expression 'pour des prunes' means 'for nothing'. Red butter sauce is also typical of this region, with its excellent red wines from Chinon and Bourgueil. Any firm white fish can be substituted for the pike.

METHOD

Soak the prunes in half the red wine overnight. Strain, reserving the wine and cut the prunes in 2-3 pieces.

For the mousseline: mince/ grind the salmon fillet in a food processor. Blend in the egg then blend in the softened butter. Season to taste with salt, pepper and nutmeg. Set the mixture in a metal bowl over a bowl of ice. Beat until well chilled, then gradually beat in the cream. Note: do not overbeat or the cream will separate. Sauté a small piece of the mousseline and taste for seasoning.

Cut a horizontal slice off the thickest part of the pike fillets and lay it beside the tail end to form a rectangle. Lay one of the rectangles on a large piece of buttered parchment paper and spread half the mousseline on top in a band 3 in/ 7.5 cm wide. Cover with the chopped prunes, add the remaining mousseline and top with the second fish fillet. Fold any overlaps of the fish fillets along the sides of the mousseline to make a neat cylinder. Wrap in the parchment paper, then in foil, tying the ends tightly. Poach in a large pan of salted water until a skewer inserted in the centre is hot to the touch when withdrawn after 30 seconds, 30–40 minutes. Let stand 10 minutes then remove the foil. Tighten the parchment and leave the ballotine to cool. It can be cooked up to a day ahead and refrigerated.

For the sauce, make fish stock: melt 2 oz/ ¼ cup/ 60 g of the butter in a large pot. Add the onions, celery, carrots, bouquet garni and garlic and cook over low heat, stirring occasionally until soft but not brown, about 20 minutes. Add the fish bones, the remaining wine and water to cover and simmer 20 minutes. Strain the stock, discarding bones and vegetables, and boil until reduced to a glaze (p. 145). In a heavy saucepan boil the reserved liquid from the prunes with the shallots, red wine vinegar and tomato purée until reduced to a glaze. Combine with the fish glaze, stir in the cream and cook for 1 minute. The glaze can be made 2–3 hours ahead.

To finish: if necessary, reheat the ballotine by rewrapping the parchment paper package in foil and heating it in boiling salted water for about 10 minutes. To finish the sauce, heat the saucepan of glaze; add the remaining butter, a few pieces at a time, whisking constantly and moving the pan on and off the heat so the sauce softens without melting to oil. Strain it and taste for seasoning.

To serve: unwrap the ballotine and cut it in ½ in/ 1.25 cm slices with a sharp knife. Coat individual plates with sauce, set a slice of ballotine on top and serve.

For the mousseline

1 lb/ 500 g salmon fillet

1 egg

1 ½ oz/ ⅓ cup/ 45 g butter, softened

salt and pepper

pinch of nutmeg

5 fl oz/ ⅔ cup/ 150 ml double/ heavy cream

Bouillabaisse

PROVENÇAL FISH STEW

⚜

3 lb/ 1.5 kg white fish, scaled, cleaned, with their heads

2 lb/ 1 kg rich fish, scaled, cleaned, with their heads

2 large crabs, or 8–10 small spider crabs, optional

1 large spiny lobster, or 8–10 small lobster tails, optional

6 fl oz/ ¾ cup/ 175 ml olive oil

2 medium onions, sliced

2 leeks, trimmed, split and sliced

2 stalks celery, sliced

a bulb of fresh fennel, sliced, or 1 tsp dried fennel seed

1 lb/ 500 g tomatoes, peeled, seeded and chopped (p. 151)

3–4 cloves garlic, crushed

bouquet garni (p. 142)

F or bouillabaisse, you need as wide a range of fish as possible, including white fish such as monkfish, mullet, bream, whiting, sea bass and John Dory, and rich fish such as conger eel and mackerel. The only bouillabaisse fish not commonly available away from the Mediterranean is scorpion-fish ('rascasse') and red gurnard ('rouget grondin'). Shellfish are not used in the traditional Provençal recipe though I have suggested adding some here. The soup is served with sauce rouille and garlic croûtes.

METHOD

Wash and pat dry the fish and cut them in chunks. Make a fish broth using the heads and tails: put them in a pan, barely cover with water, bring to the boil, cook for 15 minutes and strain. Meanwhile, marinate the fish chunks in a bowl by mixing them with the olive oil, garlic and saffron and its liquid.

If using shellfish, leave them in their shells. With a large cleaver, chop the large crabs and spiny lobster into pieces, discarding the stomach and intestinal veins of the lobster and the spongy finger-like gills of the large crabs. Chop small crabs in half and leave lobster tails whole.

Heat the olive oil in a large flameproof casserole. Add the onions, leeks, celery and fennel and sauté lightly until soft but not brown, 5–7 minutes. Add the tomatoes, garlic, bouquet garni and orange rind. Stir in the fish broth, saffron and its liquid and season with salt and pepper. Bring to the boil and simmer for 30–40 minutes. The liquid can be made up to 8 hours ahead and refrigerated.

Twenty minutes before serving, bring the liquid to the boil. Add the rich fish and shellfish and boil uncovered as hard as possible for 7 minutes. Don't stir, but shake the pan from time to time to prevent the mixture from sticking. Put the white fish on top and boil until the fish just flakes easily, 5–8 minutes, adding more water, if necessary, to cover all the pieces of fish. Note: keep the liquid boiling fast so that the oil emulsifies in the broth and does not float on the surface.

To serve: using a draining spoon, transfer the fish to a hot deep dish, arranging them so the different kinds are separated. Cover with foil and keep warm. Discard the bouquet garni and orange rind from the broth, then whisk in the tomato paste and anise liquor and taste for seasoning. Pour it into a bowl or soup tureen. Sprinkle the broth and fish with chopped parsley and serve both at the same time, leaving guests to help themselves to fish, broth, sauce rouille and croûtes.

thinly peeled strip of orange rind

pinch of saffron, soaked in 1–2 tbsp boiling water

salt and pepper

1 tbsp anise liquor

1 oz/ 30 g chopped parsley

For the marinade

3 tbsp olive oil

2 cloves garlic, finely chopped

pinch of saffron, soaked in 1–2 tbsp boiling water

For serving

sauce rouille (p. 13)

15–20 croûtes (p. 144) fried, then rubbed with a cut garlic clove

Filets de Poisson en Tapenade

FISH WITH BLACK OLIVE AND ANCHOVY SAUCE

⚜

SERVES 8

3 lb/ 1.4 kg fish fillets

3–4 tbsp olive oil

juice of 1 lemon

salt and white pepper

For the Tapenade

2 ½ oz/ ⅓ cup/ 75 g black olives, stoned/ pitted

4 anchovy fillets

2 tbsp capers, drained

3 cloves garlic, peeled

2 fl oz/ ¼ cup/ 60 ml olive oil

black pepper

U sually served with hardboiled eggs or raw vegetables, Provençal tapenade is also delicious with a full-flavoured fish such as sea bass, bream, or John Dory.

METHOD

Prepare the tapenade: put the stoned/ pitted olives, anchovy fillets, capers and garlic in a food processor or blender. Using the pulse button, gradually pour in the olive oil to form a coarse or finely chopped mixture, as you prefer. Season it to taste with pepper. Tapenade can be refrigerated, tightly covered, up to a week.

An hour or two before serving, marinate the fish: lay the fillets in a shallow dish and sprinkle them with half the olive oil, the lemon juice, salt and pepper. Cover and refrigerate them 1–2 hours, turning once or twice.

To finish: put the remaining oil in a heavy frying pan. Add the fish fillets and cover tightly. Cook over very low heat until the fish just flakes easily, 5–8 minutes, depending on thickness. Turn the fish once during cooking and do not allow it to brown. Transfer the fillets to a serving dish and spread the tapenade on top. The fish is good hot or at room temperature. (It can be kept for up to 2 hours at room temperature.)

POULTRY

Poulet au Beaujolais
———
CHICKEN WITH BEAUJOLAIS WINE AND ONIONS

⚜

SERVES 4–6
———

a 5 lb/ 2.3 kg roasting
chicken or fowl, cut in 8
pieces (p. 144)
———

2 tbsp oil
———

2 tbsp butter
———

4 fl oz/ ½ cup/ 125 ml
chicken stock (p. 150),
more if needed
———

1 clove garlic, crushed
———

2 shallots, finely
chopped
———

salt and pepper
———

24–30 baby onions,
peeled
———

kneaded butter (p. 146)
made with 3 tbsp butter,
and 3 tbsp flour
———

8–12 fried croûtes
(p. 144)
———

1 tbsp chopped parsley
(for sprinkling)
———

For the marinade
———

1 bottle (3 cups/ 750 ml)
Beaujolais wine
———

1 onion, sliced
———

T he light fruitiness of Beaujolais is clearly echoed in the sauce for this chicken. If you use red wine with a different character, you'll have an equally delicious, but different, dish.

METHOD

For the marinade: in a saucepan combine the wine, onion, carrot, celery, bouquet garni, garlic and peppercorns, bring to the boil and simmer for 5 minutes; let cool completely. Pour the marinade over the chicken, top with the oil, cover and leave at room temperature for 12 hours or in the refrigerator for 24 hours, turning the pieces occasionally.

Drain the chicken pieces and pat dry with paper towels. Strain and reserve the marinade and vegetables. In a sauté pan or shallow casserole heat half the oil and half the butter. Add the chicken pieces, skin side down, and sauté over medium heat until brown, allowing at least 5 minutes. Turn, brown the other side, and remove them from the pan.

Add the reserved vegetables and bouquet garni from the marinade and cook until slightly soft, stirring occasionally for 5–7 minutes. Stir in the marinade, bring to the boil and simmer for 5 minutes. Add the stock, garlic, shallots, salt and pepper and replace the pieces of chicken. Cover and simmer on top of the stove or in a moderate oven (No 4/ 350°F/ 175°C) until the chicken is tender, 30–45 minutes for a roasting chicken, 1–1 ½ hours for a fowl. If the pan gets dry during cooking, add more stock. Heat the remaining oil and butter in a frying pan, add the baby onions, salt and pepper,

and sauté until the onions are tender, 15–20 minutes. Shake the pan occasionally so the onions
brown evenly.

Remove the chicken pieces from the liquid and
strain it. Discard the vegetables and the bouquet
garni. Taste and, if necessary, boil the liquid until
concentrated. Whisk in enough kneaded butter so
that the sauce lightly coats a spoon. Taste it for seasoning, stir in the sautéed onions and replace the
chicken. The chicken can be prepared up to 3
days ahead and kept in the sauce in the refrigerator, or it can be frozen.

To finish: if necessary, reheat the chicken and
sauce on top of the stove. Fry the croûtes. Serve the
chicken in the casserole or on individual plates,
sprinkled with parsley and with the croûtes on
the side.

1 carrot, sliced

1 stick celery, sliced

bouquet garni (p. 142)

1 clove garlic, sliced

6 peppercorns

2 tbsp olive oil

Poule au Blanc au Salsifis

POACHED CHICKEN WITH SALSIFY AND CREAM

⚜

SERVES 4

4 lb/ 1.8 kg boiling fowl

1 onion, studded with
2 cloves

2 carrots, quartered

2 cloves garlic

bouquet garni (p. 142),
including a celery stalk
and a stem of tarragon

½ pint/ 1 ¼ cups/ 300 ml
white wine

3 ¼ pints/ 2 quarts/
2 litres chicken stock
(p. 150) or water, more if
needed

salt and pepper

2 lb/ 1 kg salsify

' **P**oule au blanc' is a favourite at Norman weddings. Salsify adds flavour without disturbing its white purity; root artichokes or quartered baby turnips may be substituted. If you use a chicken rather than a boiling fowl, reduce the cooking time to 1 hour. Rice is the traditional accompaniment, cooked if you like in some stock from the chicken.

METHOD

Truss the fowl (p. 151) and put it in a small pot so it fits quite tightly with the onion, carrots, garlic and bouquet garni. Pour in the white wine and enough chicken stock or water just to cover, add a little salt and pepper and bring to the boil. Cover and simmer over low heat, skimming occasionally until the thigh of the bird is tender when pierced with a two-pronged fork, 1 ¼–1 ¾ hours.

About a half hour before the end of cooking, peel the salsify and cut it in 2 in/ 5 cm lengths. Put it in a saucepan and add enough stock from the chicken to cover it generously. (Add more stock or water to the chicken if needed.) Cover the salsify and simmer until tender, 15–20 minutes. Drain it and add the stock back to the chicken. The chicken can be cooked up to a day ahead and refrigerated in the stock.

If necessary, reheat the bird, remove it, cover it loosely with foil and keep warm. Skim any fat from the stock, boil until it is reduced to 1 ¼ pints/ 3 cups/ 750 ml, then strain it. For the sauce: melt the butter in a saucepan, stir in the flour and cook until foaming. Whisk in the reduced stock and bring the sauce to the boil, whisking constantly until it thickens. Simmer it for 2 minutes, then add the cream and taste for seasoning. Continue simmering the sauce until it lightly coats a spoon and the flavour is concentrated and mellow, 10–15 minutes.

Meanwhile carve the chicken in 6–8 pieces (p. 144), arrange it on a serving dish, cover it tightly with foil and warm it in a low oven. Add salsify to the sauce and heat gently for 2 minutes. Coat the chicken with the sauce, spooning the salsify down one side of the serving dish. Serve immediately.

For the sauce

2 ½ oz/ ⅓ cup/ 75 g butter

1 ½ oz/ ⅓ cup/ 45 g flour

1 ¼ pints/ 3 cups/ 750 ml stock (from cooking the chicken)

12 fl oz/ 1 ½ cups/ 375 ml crème fraîche (p. 143)

or double/ heavy cream

trussing needle and string

Sauté de Poulet à la Marinière

SAUTÉ OF CHICKEN WITH CLAMS AND SAMPHIRE

⚜

SERVES 4

3–3 ½ lb/ 1.5 kg chicken, cut into 8 pieces (p. 144)

3–4 tbsp flour, seasoned with salt and pepper

1 oz/ 2 tbsp/ 30 g butter

1 tbsp vegetable oil

2 tbsp white wine

2 tbsp dry vermouth

12 oz/ 375 g samphire

12 hardshell clams, cleaned as for mussels (p. 146)

4 fl oz/ ½ cup/ 125 ml chicken stock (p. 150), more if needed

1 tbsp chopped fresh chives

salt and pepper

S hellfish and seaweed add salty emphasis to this classic chicken sauté. Mussels can be substituted for the clams, while green beans are a look-alike for samphire. A crisp potato cake is an excellent accompaniment.

METHOD

Sprinkle the chicken pieces with seasoned flour, patting them until thoroughly coated. In a sauté pan or shallow casserole heat the butter and oil. Add the chicken pieces, skin side down, and sauté over medium heat until very well browned, 10–15 minutes. Turn and brown the other side. Add the wine and vermouth to the chicken. Cover and cook until the chicken is almost tender when pierced with a fork, 20–25 minutes. If some pieces cook before others, remove them. The chicken can be cooked up to 48 hours ahead and refrigerated. Undercook it slightly to allow for reheating.

To finish: cook the samphire in boiling salted water until just tender 3–4 minutes. Drain, rinse with cold water and drain thoroughly.

If necessary reheat the chicken on top of the stove. Set the clams on top of the chicken, cover and cook until they open, about 5 minutes. Remove the chicken and clams from the pan and keep them warm.

Discard any fat from the pan, add the chicken stock and bring to the boil, stirring to dissolve the juices. If necessary, continue boiling until concentrated and slightly syrupy. Stir in the chives, then add the chicken, clams and samphire and warm for 2–3 minutes. Season with salt and pepper.

Magrets de Canard aux Cerises

DUCK BREASTS WITH CHERRIES

⚜

I like to leave the skin on duck breasts, but if you prefer very lean meat, it can be removed after sautéing. Serve them rare, just like steak, as they are tough if well done. Sour cherries are classic for this dish, so if you use sweet ones omit the sugar and add a squeeze of lemon juice, or better still a handful of fresh redcurrants.

METHOD

Stone/ pit the cherries and put them in a pan with the port and sugar. Stir, then leave 1–2 hours or until the juice runs.

To finish: simmer the cherries in their liquid until tender, 5–7 minutes. Score the skin on the duck breasts down to the meat and season both sides. Heat the butter in a heavy frying pan. Add the duck breasts skin side down and sauté briskly like a steak until most of the fat is rendered and the skin is crisp, 3–4 minutes. Turn and brown the other side, allowing 2–3 minutes for rare meat. Remove the breasts and keep warm.

Discard fat from the pan. Stir in brown sugar and cook until it begins to caramelize. Add the vinegar, standing back as it will vaporize and sting your eyes. Stir to deglaze the pan juices, then add the liquid from the cherries and the stock. Bring the liquid to the boil and stir in the arrowroot paste, adding just enough to thicken the sauce lightly. Add the cherries to reheat them and taste.

Cut each breast into thin diagonal slices and arrange them overlapping on warm serving plates. Spoon a little sauce on top, with the cherries at the side. Serve at once.

SERVES 2

8 oz/ 250 g tart cherries

8 fl oz/ 1 cup/ 250 ml port wine

1 oz/ 2 tbsp/ 30 g sugar, more if needed

2 duck breasts

salt and pepper

1 tbsp butter

1 tbsp brown sugar

2 tbsp wine vinegar

4 fl oz/ ½ cup/ 125 ml duck or chicken stock (p. 150)

1 tsp arrowroot, dissolved (p. 141) in 1–2 tbsp water

Confit de Canard

PRESERVED DUCK

⚜

SERVES 4 AS A MAIN DISH

a 4–5 lb/ 1.8–2.3 kg duck, cut into 4 pieces (p. 144)

3 tbsp coarse salt

1 tsp black pepper

2–3 sprigs fresh or dried thyme

2–3 bay leaves, crumbled

3 lb/ 1.4 kg lard, more if needed

salt and pepper

'Confit' of duck or goose, perhaps Gascony's most valuable contribution to French cuisine, may be taken off the bone and used like ham to flavour soup and vegetable dishes, or a leg may be served alone, baked in the oven so the skin is wonderfully crisp. 'Pommes Sarlardaises' – potatoes fried golden brown in goose fat and redolent with garlic – are the classic accompaniment.

METHOD

Rub each piece of duck with some of the salt and put the pieces in a bowl. Sprinkle with the remaining salt and pepper, and add the thyme and bay leaves. Cover and refrigerate, turning the pieces occasionally, for 12–24 hours, depending on how strong a flavour you want.

Wipe the duck pieces with paper towels. Heat the oven to No 2/ 300°F/ 150°C. Lay the duck pieces, skin down, in a frying pan and fry gently for 15–20 minutes so that the fat runs and they brown evenly. Pack them in a small casserole and add enough melted lard to cover them. Cover with a lid and cook in the oven until the duck is very tender and has rendered all its fat, about 2 hours. The meat should be almost falling from the bone. Let it cool slightly.

To preserve the duck: pour a layer of the rendered fat into the base of a preserving jar or small terrine. Pack the pieces of duck on top and pour over enough fat to cover them completely, adding more melted lard if necessary. Cover and refrigerate for at least a week to allow the flavour to mellow. If sealed with a cloth sprinkled with salt and tightly covered, confit will keep for several months.

To serve the confit: heat the oven to No 6/ 400°F/ 200°C. Extract the pieces of duck, wiping off excess fat, and put them in a shallow baking dish. Bake them in the oven for 5 minutes, then pour off any melted fat. Continue baking until they are very hot and the skin is crisp, 10–15 minutes.

Oie Rôtie aux Marrons et
Champignons Sauvages

ROAST GOOSE WITH CHESTNUTS AND WILD MUSHROOMS

⚜

SERVES 6–8

---

a 10 lb/ 4.5 kg goose,
with giblets

---

2 tbsp softened butter

---

salt and pepper

---

1 onion, sliced

---

1 carrot, sliced

---

2 pints/ 1 ¼ quarts/
1 ¼ litres water

---

2 lb/ 1 kg fresh
chestnuts, peeled
(p. 142)

---

16 fl oz/ 2 cups/ 500 ml
milk, more if needed

---

1 tbsp butter

---

2 lb/ 1 kg wild
mushrooms, cleaned
(p. 153) and sliced

adame Fournillon, Burgundian farmer, vintner and cook, simmers wild mushrooms in their own juices, which concentrates their flavour wonderfully. Any type of wild mushroom may be used for this outstanding Christmas dish.

METHOD

Heat the oven to No 8/ 450°F/ 230°C. Truss (p. 151) the goose. Spread the softened butter on the goose, sprinkle with salt and pepper and set the bird on its back on a rack in a roasting pan. Roast it in the oven, basting occasionally, until brown, about 40 minutes. Lower the oven heat to No 4/ 350°F/ 175°C and continue roasting, basting and pouring off excess fat, allowing 15 minutes' cooking time per pound (about 30 minutes per kilo). When the bird is done, the juices will run clear when the thigh is pricked with a skewer.

Meanwhile, make stock with the giblets: in a heavy saucepan, fry the giblets in a tablespoon of fat from the goose until very brown. Add the onion and carrot and brown them also. Pour in the water, season with salt and pepper and simmer for 1–1 ½ hours until the stock has reduced by about half and is concentrated. Put the peeled chestnuts in a pan with enough milk to cover and add the lid. Bring to the boil and simmer until almost tender, 15–20 minutes. Drain them. Spread the chestnuts around the goose about 20 minutes before it is done, and stir to coat them with the goose fat. Bake them until glazed, 15–20 minutes.

Melt the tablespoon of butter in a frying pan, add the sliced mushrooms with salt and pepper and cook, tightly covered, over very low heat until the juices run. Remove the lid, raise the heat and cook until the liquid evaporates, stirring occasionally. Cooking time varies with the type of mushroom. Make the herb butter by creaming the ingredients together with salt and pepper.

When the goose is cooked, remove it from the oven and keep it warm on a serving dish, with the chestnuts. To make the gravy, reduce the pan juices to a dark-brown glaze (p. 145) and pour off the fat. Strain in the stock and bring to the boil stirring to deglaze (p. 144) the pan juices. Strain the gravy into a saucepan, bring it back to the boil and taste.

Meanwhile, warm the mushrooms over low heat. Toss them with the herb butter and taste for seasoning. Discard trussing strings from the goose, and carve the bird at the table, surrounding by the glazed chestnuts. Serve the gravy and the mushrooms separately.

For the herb butter

4 oz/ ½ cup/ 125 g butter

2 shallots, very finely chopped

1 garlic clove, very finely chopped

2 tbsp finely chopped parsley

trussing needle and string

Douillons de Pigeon aux Pommes

PIGEON DUMPLINGS WITH APPLES

⚜

SERVES 4

2 pigeons

1 ½ oz/ 3 tbsp/ 45 g
unsalted butter

salt and pepper

2 tart apples, peeled
and cored and cut in
¼ in/ 6 mm wedges

1 tbsp sugar

1 egg, beaten to mix
with ½ tsp salt (for
glaze)

Pâte feuilletée

8 oz/ 1 cup/ 250 g
unsalted butter

8 oz/ 2 cups/ 250 g flour

1 tsp salt

4 fl oz/ ½ cup/
125 ml water

F or this tasty dumpling, pigeon or quail are roasted until just rare and still juicy. (Use raised, not wild, birds otherwise they may not be tender.) Then the meat is taken off the bone, sliced and layered with apple before wrapping in puff pastry – a contemporary notion which echoes the fruit-flavoured meat pies of medieval days.

METHOD

Make the pâte feuilletée (p. 148) and chill for at least 30 minutes. Preheat the oven to No 10/ 500°F/ 260°C. Spread the pigeons with 1 tablespoon of the butter, sprinkle with salt and pepper and set them in a roasting pan. Roast them in the heated oven until browned but still pink when the breast is pierced with a skewer, 15–18 minutes. During roasting, baste them occasionally and turn them from one side on to the other and finally on to their backs. Let them cool. Remove from the pan. Discard the fat, add a few tablespoons of stock to the pan and boil, stirring to dissolve the pan juices. Return to the remaining stock.

Melt the remaining butter in a frying pan and add the apples. Sprinkle them with half the sugar and turn them over. Sprinkle with the remaining sugar and fry briskly until brown, about 5 minutes. Turn, brown the other side and let them cool.

Cut the legs from the pigeons and cut off the thigh meat. Cut the meat from each side of the breast in one piece and cut the breasts in 3–4 diagonal slices. With a cleaver chop the carcasses in pieces. Simmer the carcasses and leg bones with the stock until well reduced, ¾–1 hour.

Roll the pâte feuilletée dough to a 16 in/ 40 cm square. Trim the edges and cut into 4 equal squares. Arrange half the apple slices diagonally on each square, working from the centre so that 4 triangles of uncovered dough are left surrounding the apples. Top the apples with half the pigeon slices, then add remaining apples and pigeon on top, mounding them well. Sprinkle a little salt and pepper between each layer. Brush the edges of dough with egg glaze. Fold the dough over the filling, pinching the edges in the shape of a cardinal's hat. Pierce the top of each dumpling with a skewer and insert a foil chimney in each hole to allow the steam to escape during baking. Brush the dough with glaze and chill the dumplings until firm, at least 30 minutes. They can be refrigerated up to 8 hours.

To finish: heat the oven to No 7/ 425°F/ 220°C. Bake the dumplings on a baking sheet until puffed and brown and a skewer inserted in the centre is hot to the touch when withdrawn after 30 seconds, 30–40 minutes. If the dumplings brown too quickly, lower the oven heat to No 5/ 375°F/ 190°C and cover them loosely with foil. For the sauce, strain the stock into a small saucepan and bring to the boil with the Armagnac. Whisk in enough dissolved arrowroot to thicken the sauce lightly and taste it for seasoning. Remove the foil chimneys and pour some sauce in each dumpling.

For the sauce

16 fl oz/ 2 cups/ 500 ml brown stock (p. 149)

2 tbsp Armagnac

2 tsp arrowroot dissolved (p. 141) in 2 tbsp water

Faisan en Cocotte Vigneronne

PHEASANT EN COCOTTE WITH RED AND GREEN GRAPES

⚜

SERVES 4

8 tear-shaped fried
croûtes (p. 144)

2 pheasants weighing
about 1½ lb/ 750 g each,
with giblets

salt and pepper

2 thin slices of pork fat,
or 4 slices streaky bacon

2 oz/ ¼ cup/ 60 g butter

1 tsp marc or brandy

1 bunch watercress

For the sauce

6 oz/ 175 g seedless
green grapes

6 oz/ 175 g seedless red
grapes

8 fl oz/ 1 cup/ 250 ml
Chardonnay or full
bodied white wine

1 ½ fl oz/ 3 tbsp/ 45 ml
marc or brandy

8 fl oz/ 1 cup/ 250 ml
white veal or chicken
stock (p. 150)

rapes and pheasant share the same season, so why not the same pot?

METHOD

Preheat the oven to No 6/ 400°F/ 200°C. Fry the croûtes. Sprinkle the birds inside with salt and pepper and truss them (p. 151). Cover the breasts with the fat or bacon and tie it on with kitchen string. Heat 1 ½ oz/ 3 tbsp/ 45 g butter in a flame-proof casserole and brown the pheasants thoroughly on all sides, for about 8–10 minutes. Add the giblets, including the liver, and cover the casserole. Cook in the oven for 25–30 minutes until the juices from the centre run pink rather than red. If you prefer the birds well done, or if they are tough, continue cooking until the juice runs clear and they are tender when pierced with a skewer.

After 10 minutes, remove the pheasant liver from the casserole, let it cool, and crush it with the remaining butter using a fork. Season it with the teaspoon of marc or brandy, salt and pepper and spread it on the croûtes. For the sauce, put the grapes in a pan with the wine and simmer them for 3–5 minutes until they are lightly cooked but not soft.

When the pheasants are cooked, pour off any excess fat, add the 1 ½ fl oz/ 3 tbsp/ 45 ml marc or brandy to the pan and flame (p. 145) it. Remove the pheasants from the pot, discard the fat or bacon and remove the trussing strings. With poultry shears or a heavy knife cut along each side of the backbone and remove it. Trim the leg bones to neaten them and cut the birds in half along the breastbone. Keep them warm.

Add the wine from cooking the grapes to the pot and boil it for about 2 minutes, stirring to dissolve the pan juices. Add the stock, bring it to the boil and strain the sauce. Reduce, if necessary, to concentrate the flavour. If the pheasant is well done, it can be stored for up to 2 days in the refrigerator with the sauce, keeping the garnish separate. If you like the bird rare, however, it should be cooked at the last minute and served immediately.

To finish: if necessary reheat the pheasants in the sauce on top of the stove, adding more stock if necessary to keep them moist. Arrange the pheasant pieces on a serving dish so they overlap and keep them warm. Mix the arrowroot paste if it has separated and whisk enough into the boiling sauce so it lightly coats a spoon. Add the grapes to the sauce, bring it just to the boil and spoon the sauce over the pheasant. Garnish the dish with croûtes and watercress.

2 tsp arrowroot dissolved (p. 141) in 2 tbsp water

salt and pepper

trussing needle and string

Cailles à la Camarguaise

QUAIL WITH RICE PILAF

⚜

SERVES 4

8 quail

8 quail livers or
2 chicken livers, cut in
8 pieces

salt and pepper

3 oz/ 6 tbsp/ 90 g butter

8 oz/ 250 g lean bacon
or Canadian bacon, cut
in lardons (p. 146)

8 fl oz/ 1 cup/ 250 ml
white wine

1 pint/ 2 ½ cups/ 600 ml
chicken or veal stock
(p. 150)

1 ¼ cups/ 225 g rice

bouquet garni (p. 142)

1 lb/ 500 g chipolata or
baby frankfurter
sausages

pinch of cayenne pepper

1–2 tbsp butter, to finish

string

R ice has been grown for centuries in the Camargue, the warm wet delta of the Rhône. Here it is cooked as a pilaf with quail, which thrive on the herb-scented inland hillsides.

METHOD

Clean the quail and put the livers inside the bodies. Sprinkle with salt and pepper and tie them with string. Heat the oven to No 4/ 350°F/ 175°C.

Heat one-third of the butter in a large casserole and fry the bacon until lightly browned. Remove the bacon, add the quail and brown them on all sides, 5–7 minutes. Remove them, drain off all the fat, add the wine and boil until reduced to 2 fl oz/ ¼ cup/ 60 ml. Add the stock and bring to the boil, then add the rice, bacon, bouquet garni, salt and pepper, spreading the rice so it is covered by stock. Cover and bake in the oven 10 minutes.

Add the quail and continue cooking until all the stock is absorbed by the rice and no pink juice runs from the cavity of the quail when they are lifted with a fork, 8–10 minutes. If the rice is not tender, remove the quail, add a little more water to the rice and continue cooking it.

To finish: heat half the remaining butter in a saucepan and sauté the sausages. Reheat the quail and rice on top of the stove, if necessary. Remove the quail, discard the strings and keep them warm. Discard the bouquet garni and season the rice with the salt, pepper and cayenne. Stir to separate the grains and dot with the remaining butter. When it has melted, pile the rice on a platter and arrange the quail and sausages around them.

MEAT AND GAME
⚜

La Daube de Boeuf de Madame Caizac

BEEF STEW WITH OLIVES

⚜

3 lb/ 1.4 kg beef chuck or round roast, cut in 2 in/ 5 cm cubes

12 oz/ 375 g lean bacon, cut into lardons (p. 146)

12 oz/ 375 g lean salt pork, cut into lardons

4 tbsp olive oil

2 onions, sliced in thick rounds

2 carrots, sliced in thick rounds

6 ½ oz/ 1 cup/ 200 g black and/ or green olives, stoned/ pitted

1 ½ pints/ 3 cups/ 750 ml brown stock (p. 149), more if needed

salt and pepper

8 oz/ 250 g mushrooms, sliced

kneaded butter (p. 146) made with 3 tbsp butter and 3 tbsp flour

M adame Caizac, proprietress of La Terrine Gourmande in Apt, makes several changes to the traditional Provençale daube. She uses beef rather than lamb and likes to brown the meat before adding wine, so the sauce is more succulent. She also adds white rather than red wine, and does not bother with tomatoes. Fresh noodles (p. 99) are the best accompaniment.

METHOD

In a bowl, combine the marinade ingredients except the oil. Add the beef, stir well, and pour the olive oil on top. Cover and leave to marinate for 1–2 days in the refrigerator, turning the beef occasionally. Blanch (p. 141) the bacon and salt pork, drain, rinse under cold running water and drain thoroughly. Preheat the oven to No 2/ 300°F/ 150°C.

Remove the beef and strain the marinade. Chop the garlic and tie the herbs and peppercorns in a piece of muslin/ cheesecloth. Pat the meat dry on paper towels. In a heavy casserole, heat half the oil and brown the meat very thoroughly on all sides over high heat. You may have to do this in several batches. Remove the meat, add the onions and brown them also. Add the reserved marinade to the casserole and stir to deglaze (p. 144) the pan. In layers, add the beef, bacon, salt pork, carrots and olives, with the garlic and the bag of herbs. Add enough stock to just cover the meat, with some pepper. Note: the bacon and olives will add salt. Cover and cook the daube in the heated oven until the beef is tender enough to crush in your fingers, 2–3 hours. Stir the daube from time to time and add more stock if it seems dry.

At the end of cooking, discard the herb bag. Sauté the mushrooms in the remaining oil until tender and stir into the daube. Add the kneaded butter in small pieces, shaking the pan so the butter melts into the sauce and thickens it. Simmer the sauce 2 minutes and taste it. Serve the daube from the casserole; it can be made up to 2 days ahead and kept covered in the refrigerator.

For the marinade

2 bay leaves

2–3 sprigs of thyme

2–3 sprigs of rosemary

2 tsp juniper berries

3 sprigs of parsley

10 peppercorns

2 cloves garlic, peeled

1 bottle (3 cups/ 750 ml) dry white wine

2 tbsp olive oil

muslin/ cheesecloth

Fricandeau de Veau à l'Oseille

FRICANDEAU OF VEAL WITH SORREL

⚜

SERVES 8

2 ½–3 lb/ 1.25 kg rump of veal

8 oz/ 250 g pork or bacon fat, cut in lardons (p. 146)

4–5 slices fat bacon

2 carrots, thinly sliced

2 onions, sliced

6 fl oz/ ¾ cup/ 175 ml white wine

16 fl oz/ 2 cups/ 500 ml brown stock (p. 149), more if needed

bouquet garni (p. 142)

salt and pepper

For the sorrel purée

1 ½ lb/ 750 g sorrel

1 oz/ 2 tbsp/ 15 g unsalted butter

4 fl oz/ ½ cup/ 125 ml double/ heavy cream

string

T he lemony bite of sorrel combines well with rich fish like shad, with venison, and with this braised veal. A mixture of spinach and watercress leaves can be used instead of sorrel. Fricandeau is a firm cut from the rump which holds up well to long cooking.

METHOD

Heat the oven to No 3/ 325°F/ 160°C. To lard the veal roast pierce the meat with the point of a very sharp knife and insert lardons into each cut. Tie the roast in a neat cylinder with string. Lay the bacon slices in the bottom of a casserole just big enough to contain the veal. Add the carrots and onions, set the veal on top, pour over the wine and simmer until reduced by half. Add enough stock to just cover the meat, the bouquet garni, salt and pepper. Cover the pan and bring to the boil. Cook the veal in the heated oven until very tender, 1 ½–2 hours. It can be cooked up to 48 hours ahead and refrigerated.

For the sorrel purée: wash the sorrel thoroughly and pick over it, discarding the stems. Pack it in a large pan, add a little salt, cover and cook over high heat until the sorrel is wilted, 3–5 minutes, stirring once or twice. Drain it. Melt the butter in a pan, add the sorrel and cream and cook, stirring, until the sorrel thickens to a purée which just falls easily from the spoon, about 5 minutes. The purée can be prepared up to 6 hours ahead and kept covered.

To finish: heat the oven to No 6/400°F/200°C. Reheat the meat on top of the stove, if necessary. Transfer it to a carving board, discard the strings and keep warm. Boil the cooking liquid until reduced to about 1 cup. Carve the veal in ¾ in/ 2 cm slices, set them in a shallow baking dish and spoon over the cooking liquid. Cook the veal in the heated oven, basting often, so that the liquid evaporates and the meat becomes coated with a shiny glaze.

Reheat the sorrel purée, if necessary. Pile the purée down the centre of a serving dish and arrange the veal slices overlapping on top. Spoon over any remaining cooking liquid and serve.

Jarret d'Agneau en Gasconnade

SHANK ENDS OF LAMB WITH ANCHOVY, GARLIC AND TOMATO

⚜

SERVES 10–12

2 shank ends of lamb leg (about 3 lb/ 1.4 kg each)

salt and pepper

2 tbsp olive oil

4 onions, sliced

3 carrots, sliced

white part of one leek, sliced

1 turnip, sliced

3 tbsp flour

12 anchovy fillets, chopped

1 tbsp tomato purée/ paste

1 bottle (3 cups/ 750 ml) full-bodied red wine such as Cahors

14 cloves garlic, peeled

3 tomatoes, peeled, seeded and chopped (p. 151)

bouquet garni (p. 142)

water, if needed

S low cooking is of the utmost importance for this braised lamb, a version of an ancient Gascon recipe.

METHOD

Preheat the oven to No 3/ 325°F/ 160°C. Sprinkle the lamb with salt and pepper. Heat the oil in a large heavy casserole and brown the lamb thoroughly on all sides. Take the meat out and discard all but 2 tablespoons of the fat. Add the onion, carrot, leek and turnip and cook them, stirring occasionally, until soft. Stir in the flour, anchovy and tomato purée/ paste and cook 1 minute. Add the wine, bring to the boil and simmer for 10 minutes.

Stir in the garlic, tomatoes, bouquet garni, salt and pepper and replace the lamb shanks. If necessary, add water so they are completely covered. Add the lid and cook the shanks in the oven for 3–4 hours until very tender (test with a two-pronged fork). Stir and turn the lamb from time to time during cooking and add more water if it looks dry. At the end of cooking, discard the bouquet garni and season the sauce to taste. It should be dark and rich but if it is thin, boil to reduce and concentrate it.

The shanks can be stored up to 3 days in the refrigerator, or they may be frozen. Serve them in the casserole, with boiled, fresh noodles (p. 99).

Steak aux Cinq Poivres

STEAK WITH FIVE PEPPERS

⚜

A version of the traditional 'steak au poivre', this recipe calls for five different types of pepper. It is the fifth, spicy Szechuan pepper which adds such character so use more or less to your taste.

METHOD

Toast the Szechuan pepper in a small dry pan over low heat, tossing and stirring the pepper, until it smells aromatic, 3–5 minutes. Mix it with the other peppercorns, put them in a double thickness of plastic bags and crush them finely with a rolling pin. Spread the pepper in a shallow dish, add the steak and coat it on both sides with pepper, pressing in the crushed grains. Cover and leave for up to 6 hours in the refrigerator.

If you like strong flavour, leave the peppercorns; for milder taste, scrape most of them from the meat. Sprinkle the steak on both sides with a little salt. Heat the oil in a heavy pan, add the steak and cook over medium heat until very brown, 3–4 minutes. Turn and brown the other side, allowing 3–4 minutes longer for rare steak, or 5 minutes for medium done meat. Rare meat will feel spongy when pressed with your fingertip and the meat will be resilient when medium done.

Add brandy to the pan and flame (p. 145) the steak. Transfer it to a carving board and keep warm. Add cream to the pan and boil it, stirring to dissolve the pan juices. Taste the sauce for seasoning. Carve a large steak in thick diagonal slices and arrange them overlapping on warm plates; leave individual steaks whole. Spoon the sauce over the steak and serve at once.

SERVES 2–3

1 tbsp Szechuan pepper

1 tbsp black peppercorns

1 tbsp white peppercorns

1 tbsp dried pink peppercorns

1 tbsp dried green peppercorns

1 ½ lb/ 750 g rump/ sirloin steak, cut 1 inch/ 2.5 cm thick

salt

1 tbsp oil

2–3 tbsp brandy

8 fl oz/ 1 cup/ 250 ml double/ heavy cream

Ragoût d'Agneau aux Navets

RAGOÛT OF LAMB WITH TURNIPS

⚜

SERVES 6

---

4 lb/ 1.8 kg boneless
lamb shoulder or breast

---

2 tbsp oil

---

1 ½ lb/ 750 g onions,
sliced

---

1 tbsp flour

---

6 fl oz/ ¾ cup/ 175 ml
white wine

---

12 fl oz/ 1 ½ cups/
375 ml brown stock
(p. 149), more if needed

8–10 cloves garlic,
halved

---

2 large tomatoes,
peeled, seeded and
chopped (p. 151)

---

bouquet garni (p. 142)

---

salt and pepper

---

1 lb/ 500 g turnips

T his ragoût of Languedoc lamb, fragrant from grazing the wild herbs which blanket the granite hillsides, is a winter dish, at its best when lamb is mature and full of flavour. Root celery or artichoke bottoms may be substituted for the turnips. Rice would be an appropriate accompaniment.

METHOD

Trim the excess fat from the meat and cut it into 2 in/ 5 cm chunks. Heat the oil in a heavy casserole, add the meat and brown it well on all sides over fairly high heat. Remove the meat, add the onions and cook over a low fire, stirring often, until soft but not brown, about 10 minutes. Sprinkle the onions with the flour and continue to cook until brown, 2–3 minutes. Stir in the wine and stock, return the meat to the casserole and add the garlic, tomatoes, bouquet garni, salt and pepper. Bring to the boil, cover and simmer for 30 minutes on top of the stove or in a moderate oven (No 4/ 350°F/ 175°C).

While the meat is simmering, peel and trim the turnips. Cut medium turnips in quarters and smaller ones in half. Add them to the meat and simmer an hour longer or until the meat and turnips are tender. Stir occasionally and if the stew becomes dry, add more stock. Skim off any excess fat and discard the bouquet garni; taste for seasoning. Serve the ragoût directly from the casserole. It can be refrigerated up to 3 days, or frozen, and flavour improves on reheating.

Ragoût de Porc aux Lentilles

STEWED PORK WITH LENTILS

✤

F rançoise Samson, a Norman countrywoman and dear friend, likes to stew lentils with fresh pork rather than the more common 'petit salé' salt-cured pork. Spicy sausages add piquancy, while apple sauce and crisp fried potatoes would be the local choice as accompaniment.

METHOD

Preheat the oven to No 3/ 300°F/ 150°C. Sprinkle the pork generously with salt and pepper. In a flameproof casserole heat the lard and fry the pork over high heat, a few pieces at a time, until browned on all sides, and set them aside. Then brown the sausages and set them aside. Add the onions to the pan and fry gently until brown, stirring occasionally. Add the pork with the garlic, bouquet garni, thyme, salt and pepper and enough water to cover. Cover tightly and cook in the heated oven for 30 minutes.

Meanwhile, pick over the lentils, discarding any stones, and wash them thoroughly. Stir them into the pork with water to cover by ½ in/ 1.25 cm. Cover and continue cooking, stirring occasionally, until both pork and lentils are tender, 40–50 minutes. Stir the lentils from time to time, and add more water if they are dry. At the end of cooking they should be moist but not soupy.

Ten minutes before the end of cooking, immerse the sausages in the lentils so they heat thoroughly. Before serving, discard the thyme and bouquet garni and taste the lentils for seasoning. The dish can be refrigerated up to 2 days and reheated.

SERVES 8

2 lb/ 1 kg boneless pork breast, cut in 1 in/ 2.5 cm cubes

salt and pepper

2 tbsp lard or oil

12 oz/ 375 g spicy fresh sausages such as chipolata

2 onions, chopped

6 cloves garlic, chopped

bouquet garni (p. 142)

big bunch of thyme

16 fl oz/ 2 cups/ 500 ml water, more if needed

10 oz/ 1 ½ cups/ 300 g lentils

CASSOULET

❧

SERVES 8

2 lb/ 1 kg dried white beans

salt and pepper

10 oz/ 300 g garlic poaching sausage

7 oz/ 200 g pork rind (optional)

1 lb/ 500 g bacon or salt pork, cut in lardons (p. 146)

1 ½ lb/ 750 g lamb breast

3 lb/ 1.5 kg lamb shoulder, boned

¼ cup/ 60 g goose or duck fat or lard

10 oz/ 300 g baby onions

1 ½ lb/ 750 g pork loin, cut in 2 in/ 5 cm cubes

10 oz/ 300 g saucisses de Toulouse

2 lb/ 1 kg tomatoes, peeled, seeded and coarsely chopped (p. 151)

6 fl oz/ ¾ cup/ 175 ml white wine

T he ultimate one-pot meal, cassoulet is a stew of white kidney beans, enriched with pork, pork sausages, and if you like a bit of lamb or game. One other ingredient is indispensable – confit of goose or duck. Plump garlic sausages are popular throughout France, but Polish kielbasa sausage is a good substitute. The flavour of this dish improves on standing.

METHOD

To cook the dried beans: bring the beans to the boil with enough water to cover by 2 in/ 5 cm. Cover the pan, remove from the heat, and allow the beans to stand and soften for an hour. Drain them, put them in a pan with enough water to cover generously and bring to the boil. Cover and simmer for 25 minutes, add salt and continue to cook for another 25–30 minutes or until nearly tender. Add more water during cooking if necessary so the beans are always covered.

Meanwhile poach the garlic sausage in a pan of water for 30 minutes; drain and slice it. Blanch (p. 141) the pork rind if using, rinse it under cold running water, drain thoroughly and mince/grind it. If the bacon is very salty, blanch it also.

Preheat the oven to No 5/ 375°F/ 190°C. Trim skin and excess fat from the lamb and cut it into cubes. Heat half of the goose fat in a large heavy casserole and lightly brown the bacon and baby onions; remove them and add the remaining fat. Heat it, brown the lamb cubes on all sides and remove them. Add the cubes of pork, brown them also and remove. Lightly brown the fresh sausages in the fat and remove them.

Put the chopped tomatoes in the large casserole with the minced/ ground pork rind, white wine, stock or water, bouquet garni, garlic, tomato purée/ paste and a little salt and pepper. Bring to the boil, skimming occasionally. Cover and bake in the oven for 50–60 minutes or until nearly tender, adding more stock or water if the pan becomes dry. Cut each piece of duck confit in two and add to the tomato mixture with the fresh sausages and garlic sausage. Cover and continue to bake for 30 minutes.

Drain the beans and put in large or medium baking dishes with all the meats and the onions. The dishes should be almost full, with the meats half-covered by the beans. Taste the meat cooking liquid for seasoning and discard the bouquet garni. Ladle enough of the cooking liquid into the dishes to moisten the cassoulet well without being soupy. Sprinkle it with breadcrumbs. It can be stored up to 2 days in the refrigerator. To finish: heat the oven to No 6/ 400°F/ 200°C. Bake the cassoulet for ½–1 hour, depending on the size of the dishes, or until a golden-brown crust has formed. Serve hot from the baking dishes.

2 ⅓ pints/ 1 ½ quarts/ 1.5 litres white veal stock (p. 150) or water, more if needed

bouquet garni (p. 142)

3–4 cloves garlic, chopped

1 tbsp tomato purée/ paste

4 pieces of duck or goose confit (p. 64)

⅔ cup/ 60 g dry breadcrumbs

Choucroûte Alsacienne

SAUERKRAUT WITH PORK AND SAUSAGES

⚜

SERVES 6

3 lb/ 1.4 kg uncooked
sauerkraut

1 ½ lb/ 750 g salted or
smoked shoulder or loin
of pork

1 lb/ 500 g piece of
bacon

1 bay leaf

2 cloves

8 juniper berries

4–5 coriander seeds

2 cloves garlic

5 oz/ ⅔ cup/ 150 g
goose fat or lard

2 onions, sliced

2 lb/ 1 kg pork shank

salt and pepper

¾ pint/ 1 ¾ cup/ 400 ml
dry white wine, more if
needed, preferably
Alsatian Riesling

12–18 small potatoes

6 Strasbourg sausages
or frankfurters (1 lb/
500 g total)

muslin/ cheesecloth

 ittle baked potatoes in their jackets, not the more usual boiled ones, are the best accompaniment for this supremely Alsatian dish.

METHOD

Wash the sauerkraut under cold running water and squeeze out the excess moisture; rinse and squeeze again. Put the salted (but not the smoked) pork in a pot with the bacon, cover with water and bring to the boil. Simmer for 5 minutes and taste the water; if it is very salty, repeat the blanching process. Drain thoroughly. Cut the bacon into 6 slices. Tie the bay leaf, cloves, juniper berries, coriander and garlic in a piece of muslin/cheesecloth.

Melt all but 2 tablespoons of the goose fat in a large casserole, add the onions and cook over low heat, stirring occasionally, until they just begin to brown. Spread half of the sauerkraut over the onions; then put in the salt pork, smoked shoulder or loin, with the pork shank, bacon and spice bag on top. Season it very lightly. Cover the meat with the rest of the sauerkraut and enough wine to moisten without covering it with liquid. Spread the remaining goose fat over the top. Cut a piece of greaseproof/wax paper to fit inside the pot and place it directly on top of the sauerkraut.

Cover and simmer on top of the stove or cook in a low oven (No 2/ 300°F/ 150°C), allowing 3 hours for crunchy sauerkraut, or 5–6 hours if you like it tender. If cooking for the longer time, remove the meat from the pan after 2–2 ½ hours of cooking, then replace it to reheat 30 minutes before serving.

About an hour before the end of cooking, put the potatoes in the oven with the sauerkraut. Poach the sausages in water for 10–12 minutes. The sauerkraut can be prepared ahead and refrigerated for up to 3 days.

To finish, reheat the sauerkraut if necessary in a low oven. Discard the spice bag and taste the sauerkraut for seasoning. Carve the meat in slices. Pile the sauerkraut on a platter with the meat, sausages and potatoes on top.

Ragoût de Porc aux Poireaux

PORK STEW WITH LEEKS

❧

SERVES 6

2 lb/ 1 kg boned pork
loin

salt and pepper

3 tbsp olive oil

2 cloves of garlic, finely
chopped

8 fl oz/ 1 cup/ 250 ml
full-bodied white wine

1 lb/ 500 g tomatoes,
peeled, seeded and
chopped (p. 151)

2 lb/ 1 kg leeks

1 tbsp chopped parsley

L eeks are among the prize denizens of our garden at the Château du Feÿ, tended with care by our gardener, the almost octogenarian Monsieur Milbert. They are at their best in this ragoût with pork.

METHOD

Preheat the oven to No 4/ 350°F/ 175°C. Cut the pork into six thick steaks, discarding any string, and sprinkle them with salt and pepper. Heat the oil in a flameproof casserole with the garlic. Add the pork steaks and brown them thoroughly, allowing 4–5 minutes on each side. Add the wine and tomatoes, cover and simmer for 15 minutes. Meanwhile, trim the leeks, leaving some green top. Split them, wash them very well and slice them.

Take the pork steaks from the casserole, add the leeks with salt and pepper and stir to mix. Cover the casserole and cook gently for 5 minutes. Put the pork on top of the leeks, cover and cook in the oven for 40–50 minutes until the pork is very tender. The ragoût can be kept for up to 3 days in the refrigerator. Reheat it gently on top of the stove and serve it in the casserole, sprinkled with chopped parsley.

Caillettes aux Marrons

PORK SAUSAGEMEAT WITH CHESTNUTS

⚜

C aillettes are typical country fare, giant meatballs lightened here with chestnuts. If caul fat is not available, encircle each ball of meat with a strip of smoked bacon. Serve the caillettes hot or cold.

METHOD

Soak the caul fat in cold water for about 30 minutes to make it pliable. Heat the oven to No 5/ 375°F/ 190°C. Put the peeled chestnuts in a pan with the stock, cover and simmer them until tender, about half an hour. Drain them, allow to cool, then coarsely crumble them.

Heat half of the lard in a frying pan, add the onion and sauté until soft but not brown. Add the garlic and cook 1 minute. If the bacon is very salty, blanch it (p. 141). Mince/grind the bacon, pork and pork liver using the coarse blade of the grinder, or coarsely chop them in a food processor. Put the meats in a bowl and stir in the chestnuts, onion, garlic, parsley, thyme, allspice, nutmeg, salt and pepper. Sauté a small piece and taste for seasoning.

Drain the caul fat and spread it on a work surface. Shape the meat mixture into 6 balls, each about the size of a medium potato, and put them on the fat. Cut around each ball, leaving enough fat to fold over it. Wrap the balls and set a half bay leaf on each. Put them in a greased baking dish, packing them tightly. Melt the remaining lard and spoon it on top. Bake the caillettes, basting frequently, until crusty brown on top 40–50 minutes. The caillettes can be refrigerated up to 2 days and reheated.

SERVES 6

1 large piece of caul fat (about 4 oz/ 125 g)

8 oz/ 250 g chestnuts, peeled (p. 142)

1 ⅔ pints/ 1 quart/ 1 litre white veal stock (p. 150)

2 oz/ ¼ cup/ 60 g lard or oil

1 onion, chopped

2 cloves garlic, chopped

4 oz/ 125 g streaky bacon

8 oz/ 250 g lean pork

8 oz/ 250 g pork liver

3 tbsp chopped parsley

pinch of thyme

½ tsp each ground allspice and ground nutmeg

salt and pepper

3 bay leaves

Jambon Chablisienne

BAKED HAM WITH WHITE WINE AND CREAM

⚜

SERVES 4

2 tbsp butter

1 oz/ ¼ cup/ 30 g flour

12 fl oz/ 1 ½ cups/ 375 ml dry white Chablis wine

12 fl oz/ 1 ½ cups/ 375 ml brown stock (p. 149)

5 juniper berries, crushed

5 black peppercorns, crushed

1 tbsp tomato purée/ paste

4 shallots, finely chopped

2 ½ fl oz/ ⅓ cup/ 75 ml white wine vinegar

4 fl oz/ ½ cup/ 125 ml crème fraîche (p. 143) or double/ heavy cream

salt (optional)

4 thick slices mild cooked country ham, weighing about 1 ½ lb/ 750 g

1 tbsp mixed chopped tarragon and parsley

[A] piquant mix of ham baked in a sauce of juniper berries, shallots, and white Chablis wine, brilliant with paprika and tomato.

METHOD

In a saucepan, melt the butter, whisk in the flour and cook until foaming. Whisk in the wine, stock, juniper berries, peppercorns, tomato purée/ paste, and half the shallots. Bring to the boil, stirring until the sauce thickens. Simmer for 10 minutes.

In a heavy pan, boil the vinegar with the remaining shallots until reduced to 1 tablespoon. Whisk in the wine sauce and simmer until the sauce is well flavoured and lightly coats a spoon, 5–10 minutes. Strain, whisk in the crème fraîche and add salt to taste. Note: the ham may be salty, so salt may not need to be added. The sauce can be kept in the refrigerator for up to 2 days.

To finish, preheat the oven to No 4/ 350°F/ 175°C. Arrange the ham in a shallow, heatproof dish and pour over the sauce to coat it completely. Cover with foil and bake in the oven until hot and bubbling, 15–20 minutes. Sprinkle with the herbs and serve.

Huîtres aux Crépinettes

OYSTERS WITH SPICED SAUSAGES

🔱

A round Bordeaux little sausages, hot in both senses of the word, are the traditional accompaniment to oysters on the half shell. The bother of stuffing sausage casings is avoided if you make 'crépinettes' or little cakes of sausagemeat wrapped in caul fat. Eat them with your fingers, between mouthfuls of oyster and chilled white wine. Lacy caul fat from the lining of cow's stomach is available at good butchers; otherwise, simply roll the patties in flour.

METHOD

Soak the caul fat in cold water for about 30 minutes to make it pliable. Heat 1 tablespoon of the lard in a frying pan, add the onion and cook gently until soft but not brown. Add the garlic and cook ½ minute. In a bowl mix the minced/ ground pork and pork fat. Stir in the onion, garlic, parsley, thyme, bay leaf, nutmeg, hot pepper, pepper and salt. Beat the mixture with a wooden spoon until it holds together, 2–3 minutes. Sauté a small piece and taste for seasoning.

Drain the caul fat, spread it on a work surface and cut it into 24 rectangles. Divide the meat mixture into 24 balls, and shape each into a cylinder. Wrap each cylinder in caul fat. Put them in a greased baking dish and spoon over the remaining lard. The crépinettes can be refrigerated up to 24 hours.

To finish: preheat the oven to No 5/ 375°F/ 190°C. Bake the crépinettes, basting frequently, 15–20 minutes or until well browned. Serve very hot, with the chilled oysters.

SERVES 8

8 servings of shelled/shucked oysters on the half shell, on ice

For the crépinettes

about 4 oz/ 125 g piece of caul fat

2–3 tbsp melted lard

1 onion, chopped

2 cloves garlic, chopped

1 ½ lb/ 750 g lean pork, minced/ground

8 oz/ 250 g pork fat, minced/ ground

3 tbsp chopped parsley

pinch of thyme

½ bay leaf, crumbled

pinch of grated nutmeg

¼ tsp ground hot pepper, or to taste

1 tsp peppercorns, coarsely crushed

1 tsp salt

Gigot de Chevreuil à l'Alsacienne

LEG OF VENISON WITH CRANBERRIES

⚜

SERVES 4

a leg of venison (7–8 lb/
3.5–4 kg)

8 oz/ 250 g fresh or
frozen cranberries

4 fl oz/ ½ cup/ 125 ml
water

8 oz/ 1 ¼ cups/ 250 g
sugar

1 ½ oz/ 3 tbsp/ 45 g lard
or oil

8 fl oz/ 1 cup/ 250 ml
brown stock (p. 149), or
water

4–5 tbsp 'quetsche'
plum brandy, or kirsch

8–10 fried croûtes
(p. 144), in 2 ½ in/ 6 cm
rounds

T he Vosges mountains are famous for berries as well as game. In this recipe, cranberries replace the wild bilberries/huckleberries native to Alsace. Serve the venison rare or pink, as the meat is tough if well done. The twisted, chewy pasta called 'spaëtzle' is ideal with venison, as is a purée of chestnuts or root celery.

METHOD

In a saucepan, combine the marinade ingredients, bring to the boil, simmer for 5 minutes and let cool completely. Put the venison in a deep dish just large enough to hold it and pour the cold marinade over it. Cover and leave to marinate for 1–3 days in the refrigerator, turning the meat occasionally. Lift the haunch out and pat dry with paper towels, reserving the marinade. Strain the marinade. With a cleaver trim off the shank bone and chop it in pieces.

To cook the cranberries: in a saucepan, mix the berries, water and sugar. Simmer uncovered, stirring occasionally, until the berries soften and begin to burst, 8–10 minutes. Taste, adding more sugar if necessary. The cranberries can be cooked up to 24 hours ahead.

Heat the oven to No 6/ 400°F/ 200°C. In a roasting pan, heat the lard, add the venison and baste with the hot fat. Add the chopped bones, 8 fl oz/ 1 cup/ 250 ml of the marinade and half the stock. Roast in the heated oven until medium rare and a meat thermometer registers 125°F/ 51°C, ¾–1 hour. Baste often during roasting and add more marinade if the pan gets dry. Heat the plum brandy or cognac in a small saucepan, flame it and pour it while still flaming over the venison. Transfer the venison to a serving dish and keep warm.

Meanwhile, boil the remaining marinade in a pan, skimming off the foam, until reduced to 8 fl oz/ 1 cup/ 250 ml. Fry the croûtes. When the venison is done, reduce the pan juices to a glaze (p. 145). Add the reduced marinade and the remaining stock and reduce to about 8 fl oz/ 1 cup/ 250 ml. Strain, stir in a quarter of the cranberries and purée the sauce in a food processor, or work it through a sieve. Taste, adding more brandy, sugar, salt or pepper if needed.

To serve: arrange the croûtes around the venison on the serving platter and top them with the remaining cranberries. Spoon a little sauce over the venison and serve the rest separately.

For the marinade

1 bottle (750 ml) red wine

white part of 2 leeks, sliced

4 carrots, sliced

2 onions, sliced

2 stalks celery, sliced

head of garlic, halved crosswise

2 tbsp vegetable oil

bouquet garni (p. 142)

salt and white pepper

Marcassin au Genièvre et
Champignons Sauvages

WILD BOAR WITH JUNIPER BERRIES AND WILD MUSHROOMS

✠

SERVES 4

4 wild boar noisettes, cut 1 ½ in/4 cm thick

4 oz/125 g wild mushrooms, cleaned (p. 153) and sliced

4 fried croûtes (p. 144), in rounds slightly larger than the noisettes

bunch of watercress (for garnish)

For the marinade

2 tbsp oil

1 onion, sliced

1 carrot, sliced

2 shallots, sliced

1 stalk celery, sliced

16 fl oz/ 2 cups/ 500 ml red wine

1 tsp peppercorns

2 tsp juniper berries, crushed

bouquet garni (p. 142)

1 tbsp vinegar

G olden 'chanterelles' and their cousin 'trompettes de mort', so–called because of their black colour, are relatively common, but for this recipe any edible mushrooms may be used. If wild boar proves difficult to find, you may substitute noisettes of pork – after being marinated for a day or two you'll be surprised how closely they resemble the real thing.

METHOD

For the marinade: heat the oil in a saucepan, add the onion, carrot, shallots and celery, and cook slowly until soft but not brown. Add the wine, peppercorns, juniper berries, and bouquet garni, bring to the boil, and simmer until the vegetables are tender, about 30 minutes. Leave until cold and add the vinegar.

Put the wild boar noisettes in a deep dish just large enough to hold them and pour the cold marinade over them. Cover and leave in the refrigerator 1–2 days. The longer the meat is marinated, the stronger the gamey flavour.

Lift the meat out and pat dry with paper towels; reserve the marinade. For the sauce: in a saucepan melt half the butter. Whisk in the flour and cook slowly, stirring constantly until golden brown. Stir in the marinade, the juniper berries and all but ½ cup of the stock. Bring to the boil, stirring, and simmer over low heat for 1 hour, stirring occasionally. The sauce can be prepared up to 8 hours ahead and kept with the noisettes in the refrigerator.

To finish: put the wild mushrooms in a small

saucepan with the remaining stock. Simmer until
the mushrooms are tender and the stock has evaporated, 5–7 minutes. Heat the oil in a sauté pan.
Season the noisettes with salt and pepper and
sauté over medium heat until rare, about 4 minutes on each side. Fry the croûtes.

Set the steaks on the croûtes and discard the fat
in the pan. Pour in the crème fraîche and bring to
the boil, stirring to dissolve the pan juices. Strain
the sauce into the pan and bring to the boil again.
Stir in the mushrooms and redcurrant jelly and
taste for seasoning – pepperiness is characteristic
of the sauce. Cut the remaining butter into small
pieces and add it to the sauce off the heat, shaking
the pan so the butter is incorporated. Arrange the
steaks on individual warm plates, spoon a little
sauce on top and garnish each with watercress.
Serve the remaining sauce separately.

For the sauce

2 oz/ ¼ cup/ 60 g butter

1 oz/ ¼ cup/ 30 g flour

1 tsp juniper berries,
crushed

16 fl oz/ 2 cups/ 500 ml
brown stock (p. 149)

1 tbsp oil

salt and pepper

3 tbsp crème fraîche
(p. 143)

1 tsp redcurrant jelly

Lapin Rôti à la Moutarde de
Madame Bouterin

ROAST RABBIT WITH MUSTARD AND
TOMATOES PROVENÇALE

⚜

SERVES 6

1 rabbit (about 3 lb/
1.4 kg), cut into serving
pieces (p. 149)

6–8 tbsp mustard

3 tbsp olive oil

2 tbsp chopped basil

1 tbsp each chopped
savory and rosemary

bouquet garni (p. 142)

10 cloves garlic,
unpeeled

2 onions, finely chopped

4 fl oz/ ½ cup/ 125 ml
dry white wine

2 tbsp fresh parsley

For the tomatoes

3–4 large tomatoes

3 tbsp browned
breadcrumbs

1 clove garlic, finely
chopped

1 tbsp chopped parsley

salt and pepper

2 tbsp olive oil

F or friend and cook Marie-Thérèse Bouterin,
Provençal cooking 'is like the light, red and
yellow, explosive.' Her recipe for roast rabbit with
mustard is very much in the vivid Provençal tradition, packed with herbs and garlic.

METHOD

Preheat the oven to No 4/ 350°F/ 175°C. Generously oil a roasting pan. Brush the rabbit pieces
evenly with mustard and set them in the pan.
Sprinkle them with oil, basil, savory and rosemary
and add the bouquet garni. Roast the rabbit in
the oven until tender and golden brown, ¾–1
hour. During roasting, turn the pieces, brushing
them with more mustard and sprinkling them
often with olive oil. Add the garlic after 15 minutes.

Cut the tomatoes in half crosswise, discarding the cores. Put them in a buttered baking dish.
In a separate bowl, combine the breadcrumbs,
garlic, parsley, salt, pepper and oil, stirring to
form a crumbly mixture. Spoon it on the tomatoes
and bake them in the oven with the rabbit until just
tender, 12–15 minutes.

After roasting, remove the rabbit pieces and garlic. Add the onions to the pan and cook, stirring,
until they are golden brown, 3–5 minutes. Add
the wine to deglaze (p. 144) the pan and simmer
so it reduces well. Taste the onions for seasoning,
spoon them over the rabbit, sprinkle with parsley
and arrange the tomatoes around the dish. If
reheated, the rabbit tends to be dry but on a hot
day it is excellent cooked ahead to serve at room
temperature.

VEGETABLES AND SALADS

⚜

Aligot

POTATO AND CHEESE PURÉE

⚜

SERVES 4

2 lb/ 1 kg potatoes,
peeled

salt

2 oz/ ¼ cup/ 60 g butter

8 fl oz/ 1 cup/ 250 ml
double/ heavy cream or
crème fraîche (p. 143)

12 oz/ 4 cups/ 375 g
grated Cantal cheese

pepper

A ligot is a lighter version of fondue made with piquant Cantal cheese from the Massif Central. Sharp cheddar can be substituted. At least one restaurant I know makes the preparation of aligot a theatrical performance: a large copper pan of creamy mashed potato is heated over a burner, then little by little the grated cheese is beaten in by lifting the purée with a wooden spoon and letting it fall in great arcs back into the pan. The whole operation takes at least five minutes, leaving the waiter pink and perspiring, the diner round-eyed with suspense.

METHOD

Cut the potatoes into 2–3 chunks, put them in a pan of cold salted water, cover and bring them to the boil. Simmer until the potatoes are tender when pierced with a knife, 15–20 minutes. Note: they should be quite soft.

Drain the potatoes and, while still hot, push them through a sieve or purée in a hand food mill. Note: if you use a food processor to purée the potatoes, they will become gummy and elastic. Put the purée in a heavy saucepan, add the butter and beat the potatoes with a wooden spoon over a low fire until light and fluffy, 2–3 minutes. Gradually beat in the cream, still working over a low heat. Little by little add the cheese and continue beating constantly with a wooden spoon until the aligot forms long ribbons when it falls from the spoon. Add pepper, taste for seasoning and serve very hot. The aligot is best if served immediately, but can be kept warm over a water bath (p. 152).

Gratin de Racines d'Hiver
GRATIN OF WINTER ROOT VEGETABLES

⚜

W hen mixed with potato in this gratin, the strong flavour of roots like kohlrabi is tamed. The same trick works well with turnips, root celery and Jerusalem artichokes.

METHOD

Divide the milk between two pans, adding salt and pepper. Peel the roots, slice them thinly and add them at once to one milk pan to prevent their discolouring. Bring them to the boil and simmer until they are almost tender, 15–20 minutes depending upon the vegetable.

Meanwhile, peel the potatoes, slice them thinly and add them quickly to the other pan of milk. Bring it to the boil and simmer also until they are almost tender, 15–20 minutes. Drain both vegetables, reserving 12 fl oz/ 1 ½ cups/ 375 ml of the milk and keeping the rest for another purpose such as soup.

Rub a shallow baking dish with the garlic and then butter it. Spread half the vegetables in the baking dish and season them with salt and pepper. Add the remaining vegetables and season again. Stir the reserved milk with the nutmeg into the cream and pour it over the vegetables. Sprinkle with the grated cheese. The gratin can be prepared up to 12 hours ahead and kept in the refrigerator.

To finish: heat the oven to No 4/ 350°F/ 175°C. Bake the gratin for 25–30 minutes until it is very hot and the top has browned.

SERVES 6–8

2 pints/ 1 ¼ quarts/ 1.25 litres milk

salt and pepper

1 lb/ 500 g root vegetables

1 lb/ 500 g potatoes

1 clove of garlic, peeled

grated nutmeg

12 fl oz/ 1 ½ cups/ 375 ml crème fraîche (p. 143) or double/ heavy cream

3 oz/ 90 g grated Gruyère cheese

Galette de Pommes de Terre aux
Champignons Sauvages

POTATO GALETTE WITH WILD MUSHROOMS

⚜

SERVES 3

6 oz/ 175 g wild
mushrooms, cleaned
(p. 153)

2 ½ oz/ ⅓ cup/ 75 g
goose fat or olive oil

salt and pepper

2-3 cloves garlic,
chopped

2 shallots, chopped

2 tbsp parsley, chopped

1 lb/ 500 g potatoes,
peeled

8 in/ 20 cm heavy frying
pan

This galette was layered with fresh truffles in the days when they were cheap, but I've found other fungi, particularly cèpes, a quite acceptable substitute. Even cultivated mushrooms enliven an otherwise plain fried potato cake.

METHOD

Cut the mushrooms in large pieces. Heat 2 tablespoons of the fat or oil in a frying pan and add the mushrooms, salt and pepper. Sauté briskly, stirring, until the mushrooms are tender and all moisture has evaporated; cooking time varies with the type of mushroom. Stir in the garlic, shallots and parsley and taste for seasoning.

Preheat the oven to No 5/ 375°C/ 190°C. Cut the potatoes in ⅛ in/ 3 mm slices, if possible using a mandolin slicer or a food processor. Heat 2 tablespoons of the fat or oil in the frying pan for 1 minute. Remove and arrange half the potato slices overlapping in circles. Sprinkle them with salt and pepper and spread the mushrooms on top. Cover the mushrooms with the remaining potatoes and spoon over the remaining fat. Press a piece of foil with a weight on top.

Cook the galette on top of the stove until the underside starts to brown, 5–8 minutes. Transfer it to the heated oven and continue cooking for 15-20 minutes until the potatoes are tender.

Remove the foil and weight and flip the galette in the pan. Alternatively, slide it on to a plate, then tip it back into the pan. Continue cooking it until the underside is brown. It is best served at once, though it can also be reheated.

Pâtes Fraîches Cévenole

PASTA WITH HAM, PINENUTS AND BASIL

⚜

P inenuts add an attractive crunch to this sauce and you can use homemade or ready-prepared fresh green pasta.

METHOD

For the pasta: sift the flour on to a work surface and make a well in the centre. Beat the eggs, spinach, oil and salt together with a fork and pour into the well. Gradually draw in the flour, working the dough lightly between the fingers so it forms large crumbs, adding a little water if the crumbs are dry. Shape the dough into a ball and knead until very elastic, about 10 minutes. Cover with an upturned bowl and allow to rest for ½-1 hour.

Roll the dough out as thinly as possible. Sprinkle it with flour, roll loosely and cut into ¼ inch/ 6 mm strips as noodles. Spread them on a floured surface, tossing them until lightly coated. Leave them to dry for 1 hour, or up to 8 hours.

To finish: shred the basil, reserving 8 sprigs for garnish. Heat half the olive oil in a deep saucepan. Add the tomatoes and garlic and sauté, stirring, until slightly thickened, about 5 minutes. Add the ham and pinenuts and sauté until they are heated. Add the chopped basil and toss until mixed. Season with pepper and taste.

Bring a pan of salted water to the boil, add the noodles and cook until they are tender but still firm, about 2 minutes for fresh pasta and 5-10 minutes for prepared pasta. Drain them.

Heat the remaining olive oil in a pan, add the pasta and toss until hot, 1–2 minutes. Pile the pasta on plates, top with sauce and add a sprig of basil.

SERVES 8

large bunch (2 oz/ 60 g) fresh basil

4 fl oz/ ½ cup/ 120 ml olive oil

4 lb/ 2 kg fresh tomatoes, peeled, seeded and chopped (p. 151)

8 cloves garlic, chopped

8 oz/ 250 g smoked raw ham such as prosciutto, diced

4 oz/ ½ cup/ 125 g pinenuts, toasted

salt and pepper

For the pasta

12 oz/ 3 cups/ 375 g flour

6 eggs

1 lb/ 500 g spinach, cooked (p. 149) and finely chopped

2 tbsp oil

1 tsp salt

Feuilletés aux Asperges

ASPARAGUS WITH TARRAGON BUTTER
SAUCE IN PUFF PASTRY

⚜

SERVES 8

1 egg mixed with ½ tsp
salt (for glaze)

1 ½ lb/ 750 g asparagus

6 oz/ ¾ cup/ 180 g
chilled, unsalted butter,
cut in pieces

4 tbsp chopped tarragon

squeeze of lemon juice

salt and pepper

Pâte feuilletée

8 oz/ 2 cups/ 250 g flour

8 oz/ 1 cup/ 250 g butter

1 tsp salt

1 tsp lemon juice

4 fl oz/ ½ cup/ 125 ml
water

The soft sandy soil of the Loire valley is ideal
for asparagus. In spring, if you see a carefully tilled field that is apparently empty, you can be
sure that prized stems of white asparagus lurk
underground. As soon as they poke through, they
are snipped with a special tool 8 inches/ 20 cm
below the surface so they remain bleached. Here,
the asparagus is set in a puff pastry case and topped
with the lightest of herb sauces made only of butter whisked with chopped tarragon and a squeeze
of lemon juice. If asparagus is out of season, green
beans are an excellent alternative.

METHOD

Make the pâte feuilletée dough (p. 148) and chill
thoroughly. Roll the dough to a sheet ⅛ inch/
3 mm thick. Cut eight 4 inch/ 10 cm diamonds and
brush them with the egg glaze. With the tip of a
knife, mark a line inside each diamond to make a
lid, cutting halfway through the dough. Trace an
asparagus spear on each feuilleté. Scallop the
edges of each diamond with a knife to help rising
and transfer them to a baking sheet. Chill until
firm, about 30 minutes.

Heat the oven to No 7/ 425°F/ 220°C. Bake the
feuilletés in the heated oven 8–12 minutes. Lower
the heat to No 5/ 375°F/ 190°C and continue baking until puffed and golden, 12–15 minutes. Transfer to a rack, cut the lids from the feuilletés and
scoop out any uncooked dough. The feuilletés
can be stored 2 days in an airtight container, or
frozen.

Peel the lower part of the asparagus stems with

a vegetable peeler and trim to equal lengths. Tie them with string in 8 equal bundles. Cook the asparagus in a large pan of boiling salted water until tender but still slightly firm, 7–10 minutes. Drain it, rinse with cold water and drain again thoroughly.

Heat the oven to No 1/ 275°F/ 140°C. Warm the feuilletés on a baking sheet in the oven. If necessary, warm the asparagus in a steamer over boiling water. Cut the asparagus spears in 3 in/ 7.5 cm lengths, discarding the strings. Dice the asparagus trimmings and spread them in the feuilleté cases. Top with asparagus spears, draping them over one edge of the pastry. Half cover the feuilletés with a pastry lid to keep warm.

Make the tarragon butter sauce: put a teaspoonful of water with 2–3 pieces of butter in a small heavy pan. Heat gently, whisking constantly, until the butter softens creamily. Add the remaining butter a few pieces at a time, moving the pan on and off the heat so the sauce softens without melting to oil. Note: do not heat it above blood temperature. Whisk in the chopped tarragon and lemon juice and season to taste with salt and pepper. Serve the sauce in a bowl with the warm feuilletés.

Papeton d'Aubergines

AUBERGINE/EGGPLANT MOULD

⚜

SERVES 6–8

1 lb/ 500 g
aubergines/eggplants

6 ½ oz/ 200 g
courgettes/zucchini,
sliced in thick rounds

salt and pepper

3 tbsp olive oil

2 medium onions,
chopped

3 cloves garlic, finely
chopped

1 large red pepper,
cored, seeded and diced

1 large green pepper,
cored, seeded and diced

1 egg, beaten to mix

1 ½ oz/ ½ cup/ 45 g
breadcrumbs, more if
needed

D uring the 14th century the Catholic popes were based in Avignon and have given their name to this aubergine/eggplant terrine. For the appropriate papal tiara shape, Papeton is best cooked in a tall charlotte mould. The recipe is typical of the herb, oil and garlic-laden Provençale vegetable salads, at their best served at room temperature.

METHOD
Preheat the oven to No 7/ 425°F/ 220°C. Halve the aubergines/ eggplants lengthwise, and score the flesh with a knife. Sprinkle the aubergines/ eggplants and courgettes/ zucchini with salt and let them stand for 30 minutes to draw out the juices. Rinse both vegetables with water and pat them dry with paper towels.

Put the aubergines/ eggplants cut side down on an oiled pan and bake in the heated oven until the flesh is somewhat soft, 15–20 minutes. Remove the pulp with a spoon, being careful not to pierce the skin. Reserve the skins. In a skillet, heat 2 tablespoons of the oil and sauté the courgette/ zucchini rounds until lightly browned on both sides.

For the tomato coulis: put the tomatoes, bouquet garni, salt and pepper in a heavy-based saucepan. Cover and cook over very low heat for 10 minutes. Uncover and simmer, stirring occasionally, until very thick, about 15 minutes.

In a large heavy pan, heat the remaining oil, add the onions and cook slowly until soft but not brown. Add the aubergine/ eggplant pulp, courgettes/ zucchini, garlic, red and green peppers, and half of the tomato coulis with the bouquet garni, salt and pepper. Taste the remaining coulis and reserve it. Cook the aubergine/ eggplant mixture, uncovered in the oven, stirring occasionally, until the vegetables are tender and the mixture is thick, 25–30 minutes. Discard the bouquet garni. Remove the pan from the heat and let cool slightly. Stir in the egg and enough breadcrumbs to make the mixture stiff but not dry. Taste it for seasoning.

Preheat the oven to No 4/ 350°F/ 175°C. Oil the charlotte mould generously and line it with the aubergine/ eggplant skins, purple sides outward. Fill it with the vegetable mixture, folding any overlapping skins on top. Cover the papeton with oiled paper and set it in a water bath (p. 152). Bring it to the boil on top of the stove and bake in the oven until firm and a skewer inserted in the centre is hot to the touch when withdrawn, about 1 hour. Let the papeton cool. It can be refrigerated, with the tomato coulis, up to 2 days. Unmould it shortly before serving and serve it at room temperature, edged with the reserved tomato coulis.

For the tomato coulis

1 lb/ 500 g tomatoes, peeled, seeded and chopped (p. 151)

bouquet garni (p. 142)

salt and pepper

2 ⅓ pint/ 1 ½ quart/ 1.5 litre charlotte mould

Salade aux Haricots Blancs Languedocienne

WHITE BEAN SALAD

⚜

SERVES 6–8

For the beans

1 lb/ 500 g dried white beans

1 onion studded with 2 cloves

bouquet garni (p. 142)

1 clove garlic, cut in half

salt and pepper

For the salad

4 tbsp wine vinegar

6 fl oz/ ¾ cup/ 175 ml olive oil

1 clove garlic, finely chopped

3–4 sprigs fresh thyme, or 1 tsp dried thyme

3–4 sprigs fresh oregano, or 1 tsp dried oregano

2 medium tomatoes, peeled, seeded and chopped (p. 151)

1 shallot, finely chopped

1 small onion, cut in thin rings (for decoration)

I n summer this salad is good with cold roast lamb, or the spicy 'merguez' sausage made popular in Languedoc by the sizeable Arab population. To conform to the Islamic code, merguez are usually made with lamb, not pork.

METHOD

Put the beans in a bowl, cover them generously, with cold water and leave to soak 6–8 hours.

Drain the beans and transfer them to a large saucepan. Cover with water and add the onion studded with cloves, bouquet garni, garlic and pepper. Bring slowly to the boil and simmer until the beans are tender, 1–1 ½ hours. Add water when needed so the beans are always covered. Note: season the beans with salt only halfway through cooking or they will be tough. Drain the beans and discard the onion, bouquet garni and garlic.

Make a vinaigrette with the wine vinegar and olive oil (p. 152) and whisk in the chopped garlic. Chop half the thyme and oregano, reserving the rest for decoration. In a large bowl stir together the drained beans, tomatoes, shallot, and chopped herbs. Pour over the vinaigrette, stir and taste the salad for seasoning. Allow the salad to marinate for at least 2 and up to 24 hours before serving, so that the flavours mellow.

Just before serving, decorate the top with onion rings and herb sprigs.

Salade Lyonnaise

HOT BACON AND EGG SALAD

⚜

C hewy greens such as escarole or dandelion are best with a bacon dressing as the hot fat wilts the greens and makes them tender. The Lyonnais like to add a soft boiled egg, but sliced chicken livers or a few mushrooms are other possibilities.

METHOD

To soft boil the eggs: put them in cold water, bring to the boil and simmer them 5–6 minutes. Transfer them to a bowl of cold water and leave to cool. Tap them gently all over to crack the shells, then peel them carefully under running water. Note: the yolks should be soft in the centre. Thoroughly wash the salad greens, drain and dry them. Put them in a salad bowl. If the bacon is salty, blanch (p. 141) and drain it. The eggs, salad and bacon can be prepared up to two hours ahead.

To finish: heat the oil and fry the bacon until lightly browned but still tender. Discard the excess fat, or add more oil to make about 3 fl oz/ 6 tbsp/ 90 ml. Heat will wilt the leaves slightly. Add the vinegar to the hot pan, standing back from the fumes, and cook until it has reduced by half. Pour it over the salad and toss again. Taste for seasoning and add salt and pepper if needed.

To serve: pile the salad on 4 individual plates and set an egg on top. Serve at once.

SERVES 4

4 eggs

a medium-size head of curly endive or escarole (about 12 oz/ 375 g)

8 oz/ 250 g streaky bacon, cut in lardons (p. 146)

2 tbsp oil

3 fl oz/ 6 tbsp/ 90 ml wine vinegar

salt and pepper

Salade de Chou Rouge au Confit de Canard

RED CABBAGE SALAD

⚜

SERVES 4–6 AS AN APPETIZER

4 pieces of duck confit (see p. 64)

1 small head (about 1 lb/ 500 g) red cabbage

2 fl oz/ ¼ cup/ 60 ml red wine vinegar, more if needed

3 ¼ pints/ 2 quarts/ 2 litres water

For the vinaigrette

4 tbsp red wine vinegar

salt and pepper

1 tbsp Dijon mustard

6 fl oz/ ¾ cup/ 175 ml walnut oil

4 oz/ 1 cup/ 125 g walnuts

T he crispness of red cabbage and the melting richness of duck confit make an excellent marriage, a hearty appetizer for cold weather.

METHOD

Bake the confit in the oven until hot and crisp. Quarter the cabbage, and cut out the core. Very finely shred the leaves lengthwise with a knife to obtain long strips. Put the strips in a bowl. Bring the vinegar to the boil, pour it over the shredded cabbage and mix well. Bring the water to the boil and pour over the cabbage. Let soak until the cabbage is slightly softened, 1–2 minutes, then drain it. The cabbage can be prepared 3–4 hours ahead and kept covered at room temperature.

Make the vinaigrette dressing (p. 152). Just before serving mix the cabbage with the walnuts and enough dressing to moisten well. Taste for seasoning, adding more vinegar if necessary. Pile the cabbage on individual plates. With two forks, pull the confit from the bones into coarse shreds. Scatter the shreds over the cabbage and serve while still warm.

Salade de Choufleur, Sauce Gribiche

CAULIFLOWER WITH PIQUANT MAYONNAISE

⚜

Cauliflower and artichokes, symbols of Brittany in the world of wholesale produce, are well served with sauce Gribiche, a light mayonnaise flavoured with mustard, gherkins, capers and herbs.

METHOD

For the sauce, separate the egg whites from the yolks and coarsely chop the whites. Pound or mash the hardboiled yolks in a small bowl with the raw yolk. Gradually whisk in the oil a few drops at a time until the mixture thickens, as for mayonnaise. When the mayonnaise is thick add the white wine, then whisk in the remaining oil in a steady stream. Finally, stir in the mustard, chopped gherkins, capers, herbs and chopped egg whites and mix well. Add salt and pepper to taste.

Trim and core the cauliflower, then separate it into florets. Put the florets in a large pan of boiling salted water and simmer until tender but still firm, 5–8 minutes. Drain the cauliflower, rinse it with cold water and drain it again thoroughly.

Generously butter the custard cups. Pack the cooked florets into the moulds with the stems inward. Fill the centre with more florets, then press each lightly with a saucer. The sauce and cauliflower can be stored separately in the refrigerator for up to 24 hours. Allow the cauliflower and sauce to come to room temperature before serving.

To finish, unmould the small cauliflowers on to a platter or individual plates. Spoon over the gribiche sauce to half coat the cauliflower and garnish the top with a herb sprig.

SERVES 6

a medium (about 2 lb/ 1 kg) cauliflower

salt and pepper

For the sauce gribiche

2 hardboiled eggs

1 raw egg yolk

12 fl oz/ 1 ½ cups/ 375 ml oil

2 tbsp white wine

1 tsp Dijon mustard

1 tbsp gherkin pickles, chopped

1 tbsp capers

2 tbsp chopped mixed herbs such as parsley, chives and tarragon

herb sprigs (for garnish)

six 6 fl oz/ ¾ cup/ 175 ml custard cups

DESSERTS

Boule de Neige

CHOCOLATE SNOWBALL

⚜

C hocolate arrived early to Western France, from Mexico through Spain and the gateway of Bayonne, where chocolate remains a speciality. These snowballs are completely coated with whipped cream so the dark filling, half mousse, half fudge, comes as a surprise.

METHOD

Thoroughly butter the ramekins, line the base with greaseproof/ wax paper and butter the paper. Preheat the oven to No 4/ 350°F/ 175°C.

In a heavy pan, heat the chocolate gently with the coffee, stirring until melted. Cook, stirring until the mixture is thick but still falls easily from the spoon. Add the butter, sugar and cinnamon and heat, stirring until melted. Bring the mixture almost to the boil and remove from the heat. Whisk in the eggs, one by one.

Strain the mixture, then pour into ramekins. Set in a water bath (p. 152) and bring to the boil on top of the stove. Bake in the oven until a light crust forms on the chocolate, 15–18 minutes. Cover and refrigerate for at least 24 hours and up to a week.

To finish: not more than 2 hours before serving, run a knife around the ramekins and turn the snowballs on to individual plates, discarding the paper. Note: if the mixture sticks, scoop out and remould it on the plate. Make the crème Chantilly (p. 143), and scoop it into the pastry bag. Completely cover the chocolate moulds with tiny rosettes of cream, then top the centre of the snowballs with a single large rosette. Decorate them with a mint sprig or a candied violet and chill until serving.

SERVES 8

8 oz/250 g bitter chocolate, chopped

6 fl oz/ ¾ cup/ 175 ml strong black coffee

8 oz/ 1 cup/ 250 g unsalted butter, cut into pieces

6 ½ oz/ 1 cup/ 200 g sugar

1 tsp ground cinnamon

4 eggs

fresh mint sprigs or candied violets (for decoration)

8 ramekins (4 fl oz/ ½ cup/ 125 ml each); pastry bag and a small star tube

Crème Chantilly

16 fl oz/ 2 cups/ 500 ml double/ heavy cream

2 tbsp sugar

a few drops/ ½ tsp vanilla

Tartouillats

FRUIT FLANS IN CABBAGE LEAVES

⚜

SERVES 8

4 oz/ 1 cup/ 125 g flour

½ tsp salt

8 oz/ 1 ¼ cups/ 250 g
sugar

4 eggs

8 fl oz/ 1 cup/ 250 ml
milk

8 large rounded
cabbage leaves, with no
holes

1 lb/ 500 g black cherries
or pears

2 tbsp marc or kirsch

8 ramekins of 6 fl oz/
¾ cup/ 175 ml capacity
each

T he Auxerrois region of northern Burgundy is
the second largest producer of cherries in
France. A tattered old local cookbook includes a
curious recipe for 'tartouillats', which proves to be
a kind of cherry pie with cabbage leaves replacing
the pastry – a thoroughly modern conceit!

METHOD

Sift the flour into a bowl with the salt. Stir in the
sugar and make a well in the centre. Add the eggs
and half the milk and whisk just until the mixture
is smooth. Stir in the remaining milk to form a batter. Cover and leave the batter to stand about
½ hour. Preheat the oven to No 6/ 400°F/ 200°C.

Bring a large pan of water to boil and blanch
(p. 141) the cabbage leaves, then drain them. If the
stem ends of the cabbage leaves are large, cut
them out. Butter the ramekins and line them with
the drained cabbage leaves.

Stone/pit the cherries or peel, core and dice
the pears. Stir the fruit and marc or kirsch into the
batter and spoon the mixture into the cabbage
leaves. Trim the edges of the leaves with scissors
to leave a generous border above the ramekins. Set
them on a baking sheet and bake in the oven until
the filling is firm and the cabbage leaves are slightly brown, 25–35 minutes. The filling will puff up,
but shrink again as it cools.

Let the tartouillats cool slightly and then
unmould them onto a serving dish or individual
plates. Serve them warm or at room temperature.
They can be cooked a few hours ahead, but are best
eaten on the day of baking.

Glace aux Pruneaux à l'Armagnac

PRUNE ICE CREAM WITH ARMAGNAC

✠

A dvance planning is needed for this alcoholic ice cream, as the prunes which flavour it must be macerated in Armagnac for at least a week. Reserve the Armagnac to drink after dinner!

METHOD

To macerate the fruit: bring the water to the boil, pour it over the tea and leave to infuse 5 minutes. Strain the tea over the prunes in a bowl, cover and leave to soak for 12 hours. Drain the prunes, pack in a jar and pour over enough Armagnac to cover. Cover tightly and leave to macerate for at least a week at room temperature.

For the ice cream: make the vanilla custard sauce (p. 151), adding the cream with the milk. Strain it and chill. Drain the prunes. Purée the fruit in a food processor or blender, or work it through a sieve. There should be 8 fl oz/ 1 cup/ 250 ml of purée.

Stir the purée into the cold custard and chill until very cold. Freeze the mixture in an ice cream churn, then transfer to a bowl and put in the freezer. The ice cream can be stored for up to a month in the freezer. Let it soften in the refrigerator for 30 minutes before serving.

Makes 1 quart/ 1 ¼ quarts/ 1.25 litres

16 fl oz/ 2 cups/ 500 ml water

2 tbsp dry black tea

6 oz/ ¾ cup/ 175 g stoned/ pitted prunes

16 fl oz/ 2 cups/ 500 ml Armagnac, more if needed

Vanilla custard sauce

16 fl oz/ 2 cups/ 500 ml milk

8 fl oz/ 1 cup/ 250 ml double/ heavy cream

1 vanilla bean

7 egg yolks

5 oz/ ¾ cup/ 150 g sugar

ice cream churn

Crémets

MOULDED FRESH CHEESE

⚜

SERVES 6

16 fl oz/ 2 cups/ 500 ml
crème fraîche (p. 143) or
12 fl oz/ 1 ½ cups/
375 ml double/ heavy
cream plus 4 oz/ 125 g
cream cheese

4 egg whites

For serving

fresh raspberries or
strawberries

sugar or vanilla sugar

crème fraîche or crème
Chantilly (p. 143)

coeur à la crème mould
(1 quart/ 1 litre) capacity
or several small moulds;
muslin/ cheesecloth

C rémets or 'coeur à la crème' is a fresh cheese often moulded in a heart shape. The most delicate is based on crème fraîche, but soft cream cheese mixed with double/heavy sweet cream is an acceptable substitute. It is a summer dessert, at its best with fresh red berries, sugar and cream.

METHOD

Line the mould with muslin/ cheesecloth. In a large bowl whip the crème fraîche until it holds soft peaks. Alternatively, beat the double cream with the cream cheese. In another bowl, whip the egg whites until stiff. Stir about a quarter of the egg whites into the crème fraîche then fold the mixture into the remaining egg whites. Spoon the mixture into the mould and cover with plastic wrap. Set it on a dish and leave to drain in the refrigerator for at least 8, or up to 36 hours.

An hour or two before serving, turn the crémets out on to a serving dish. Arrange the raspberries or strawberries around the crémets. Serve it with separate bowls of sugar or vanilla sugar and the remaining crème fraîche or crème Chantilly.

Sorbet Normande

APPLE SORBET WITH CALVADOS

✣

The tarter the apples, the better the sorbet, and to extract their full flavour, in this recipe the apple cores and skins are simmered in syrup. Sugar should be added to taste: just a little if the sorbet is served in the middle of the meal, more if it is served as dessert.

Makes 3 ¼ pints/ 2 quarts/ 2 litres sorbet to serve 8–10

2 large Granny Smith apples, cut in ½ in/ 1.25 cm dice

2 ⅓ pints/ 1½ quarts/ 1.5 litres water

8 oz/ 1 ¼ cups/ 250 g sugar, or to taste

stick of cinnamon

4 fl oz/ ½ cup/ 125 ml lemon juice

5 fl oz/ ⅔ cup/ 150 ml Calvados

ice cream churn

METHOD

In a saucepan heat the apples, water, sugar and cinnamon stick, stirring occasionally until the sugar is dissolved. Cover and simmer for 10–15 minutes until the apples are softened to a pulp. Work the mixture through a sieve, reserving the cinnamon stick to use again. Stir in the lemon juice and Calvados and taste the mixture, adding more sugar if needed.

Chill the mixture, then freeze in the ice cream churn. Transfer the sorbet to a chilled container, cover and store in a freezer. Sorbet is best eaten within 24 hours. If storing longer, let it soften in the refrigerator 1–2 hours before serving.

Petits Vacherins aux Fraises

STRAWBERRY MERINGUE BASKETS

⚜

SERVES 6

4 egg whites, at room
temperature

6 ½ oz/ 1 cup/ 200 g
sugar

1 tsp vanilla extract

1 lb/ 1 qt/ 500 g
strawberries

1 pint/ 2 ½ cups/ 600 ml
vanilla ice cream

2 baking sheets; pastry
bag with ³/₈ in/ 1 cm
plain tube

Crème Chantilly

8 fl oz/ 1 cup/ 250 ml
double/heavy cream

2 tbsp sugar

1 tsp vanilla

T his recipe combines everyone's favourite ingredients – strawberries, ice cream and whipped cream – in a snowy sandwich of meringue.

METHOD

Whip the egg whites until stiff. Whisk in 4 tablespoons of the sugar, one at a time. Continue beating until the egg whites are glossy and form short peaks when the whisk is lifted, about 30 seconds. With a spatula, fold in the remaining sugar and vanilla and continue folding until the meringue forms long peaks, ½–1 minute. Heat the oven to No ½/ 250°F/ 120°C. Grease and flour the baking sheets or line them with non-stick parchment paper. Mark twelve 4 in/ 10 cm circles on the baking sheets.

Fill the pastry bag with the meringue mixture. Pipe twelve 4 in/ 10 cm rounds in a spiral inside the marked circles, or spread the meringue evenly in rounds with a metal spatula. Sprinkle with sugar and bake until crisp and dry, 1–1 ¼ hours. Leave to cool on the baking sheets. They can be stored in an airtight container for up to 2 weeks.

To finish: shortly before serving, hull the strawberries, washing them only if sandy. Make the Chantilly cream (p. 143). Put a scoop of vanilla ice cream in the centre of 6 of the meringue rounds. Surround the ice cream with strawberries, cutting them in half if they are large. Top the ice cream and strawberries with a spoonful of Chantilly cream and add a second round of meringue, pressing it down lightly. Serve at once.

Gâteau aux Poires
PEAR CAKE

⚜

I n this simple recipe, sliced pears are cooked in butter and sugar, then baked in a shallow layer of cake batter; apples or peaches do equally well. Crème fraîche, of course, is the mandatory accompaniment.

METHOD

Preheat the oven to No 4/ 350°F/ 175°C. Butter the mould. Peel, core, quarter, and cut the pears in ½ in/ 1.25 cm wedges. Melt half the butter. Add the pears and sprinkle with one third of the sugar and the lemon juice. Sauté briskly, turning the pears occasionally, until they are just tender, 7–12 minutes, depending on their ripeness. Lift out and drain them, reserving the juice.

Sift the flour and baking powder together on to a work surface. Make a well in the centre and add the remaining butter, remaining sugar, egg yolks, milk and vanilla. Mix the ingredients with your fingertips until the sugar is dissolved. Pour the mixture into the prepared mould and arrange the pears overlapping in concentric circles on top. Bake the cake in the heated oven until brown and starting to shrink at the edges, 30–40 minutes.

Meanwhile boil the reserved pear juice until reduced and syrupy. Shortly before the cake is done, brush the top with the juice and continue cooking until glazed and shiny, about 5 minutes. Let it cool a few minutes in the mould, then transfer to a rack to cool. The cake is best eaten the day of baking, but can be kept a day or two in an airtight container.

SERVES 8

2 lb/ 1 kg medium pears

3 oz/6 tbsp/ 90 g unsalted butter

8 oz/ 1 ¾ cups/ 250 g icing/ confectioner's sugar

juice of ½ lemon

8 oz/ 2 cups/ 250 g flour

1 ½ tbsp baking powder

4 egg yolks

4 fl oz/ ½ cup/ 125 ml milk

few drops/ ½ tsp vanilla

11 in/ 28 cm porcelain or metal quiche mould

Soufflé aux Poires Williams

PEAR BRANDY SOUFFLÉ

❦

SERVES 4

4 ripe dessert pears
(about 1 ½ lb/ 750 g)

juice of ½ lemon

3 tbsp 'Poire Williams'
pear brandy

8 egg whites

1 ½ oz/ 3 tbsp/ 45 g
sugar icing/
confectioner's sugar (for
sprinkling)

For thick pastry cream

6 fl oz/ ¾ cup/ 175 ml
milk

3 egg yolks

2 oz/ ⅓ cup/ 60 g sugar

½ oz/ 2 tbsp/ 15 g flour

1 tbsp cornstarch

3 ¼ pint/ 2 quart/ 2 litre
soufflé dish

S mall quantities of white alcohols add a concentrated kick to desserts. The flavour of ripe pears emerges clearly in this soufflé made with pear brandy.

METHOD

Make the pastry cream: scald the milk. Beat the egg yolks with the sugar until thick and light. Stir in the flour and cornstarch. Stir in half the hot milk and add the mixture to the remaining hot milk in the pan. Bring to the boil, whisking until the pastry cream thickens, and simmer for 2 minutes. To prevent a skin from forming, rub the surface of the hot cream with butter.

Peel and core the pears and purée them in a blender or food processor with the lemon juice. Cook the purée in a small saucepan, stirring until it is thick enough to hold a shape, 10–15 minutes. Let cool, then stir it into the pastry cream with the pear brandy. Press a piece of plastic wrap tightly on top to seal out air and chill up to 3 hours.

To finish: heat the oven to No 7/ 425°F/ 220°C. Thoroughly butter the soufflé dish. Whip the egg whites until stiff, beat in the sugar and continue beating until glossy, about 30 seconds. Meanwhile, reheat the pear cream until the mixture is hot to the touch. Fold a quarter of the meringue into the warm pear cream, mixing thoroughly, then add to the remaining meringue. Gently fold together and pour into the prepared soufflé dish.

Bake the soufflé in the heated oven until puffed and brown, 20–25 minutes. Sprinkle the top with icing/confectioner's sugar and serve at once.

Tarte aux Poires et Chocolat
CHOCOLATE PEAR TART

⚜

Pears and chocolate form a classic combination in Pears Belle Hélène, so to find pears topping chocolate in an open tart is a logical, delectable conclusion. Extra crispness is added to the crust by coating the tart tin/ pan with butter and sugar.

METHOD

Butter the tart tin generously, then sprinkle with sugar. Make the pâte brisée (p. 147) and chill it for 30 minutes. Roll out the dough to ⅛ in/ 3 mm thick and line the tart tin/ pan.

For the custard: beat the egg, egg yolk, cream and vanilla until thoroughly mixed.

Heat the oven to No 6/ 400°F/ 200°C. Sprinkle the bottom of the tart with the chopped chocolate. Peel and thinly slice the pears crosswise; flatten the slices lightly. Arrange them in a flower petal design on the chocolate so that the slices overlap. Spoon over the custard so the surface of the pears is coated. Note: the custard should be just visible between the pear slices. Sprinkle the pears with sugar.

Bake the tart well down near the base of the oven so the bottom cooks, 10 minutes. Reduce the heat to No 4/ 350°F/ 175°C and bake until the crust is brown and the custard is set, 15–20 minutes longer. If the pears are not caramelized, brown them under a hot grill/broiler for 2–3 minutes.

SERVES 8

4 oz/ 125 g semisweet chocolate, chopped

3 ripe desserts pears (about 1 lb/ 500 g)

2–3 tbsp sugar (for sprinkling)

Pâte brisée

6 oz/1 ½ cups/ 175 g flour

1 egg yolk

3 tbsp sugar

¾ tsp salt

3 ¼ oz/ 7 tbsp/ 100 g unsalted butter

For the custard

1 egg

1 egg yolk

4 fl oz/ ½ cup/ 125 ml single/ light cream

½ tsp vanilla, or 1 tsp kirsch

10–11 in/ 25–28 cm tart tin/ pan

Tarte aux Mirabelles
GOLDEN PLUM TART

⚜

Make the pâte brisée dough (p. 147) and chill 30

SERVES 6–8

2 lb/ 1 kg mirabelle plums

3 tbsp dry breadcrumbs

2 eggs, beaten to mix

2 fl oz/ ¼ cup/ 60 ml double/ heavy cream

2 oz/ ⅓ cup/ 60 g sugar

icing/ confectioners' sugar, or ground cinnamon (for sprinkling)

12 in/ 30 cm tart tin/ pan

Pâte brisée

8 oz/ 2 cups/ 250 g flour

4 oz/ ½ cup/ 125 g unsalted butter

1 egg

1 tsp salt

5–6 tbsp water

S tone fruits such as apricots and purple plums can take the place of mirabelle plums, and should be prepared in the same way. Cherries are good too and should be stoned/pitted and left whole.

METHOD

Make the pâte brisée dough (p. 147) and chill 30 minutes. Halve the plums, discarding the pits. Heat the oven to No 7/ 425°F/ 220°C. Butter the tart tin/ pan.

Roll out the pâte brisée and line the tin/ pan. Sprinkle the breadcrumbs in the pie shell and arrange the plums on top, cut side up. Bake in the heated oven for 10 minutes. Whisk together the eggs, cream and sugar and pour the mixture over the plums. Lower the oven to No 4/ 350°F/ 175°C and bake the pie until the dough is browned, the fruit is tender and the cream mixture is set, 40–45 minutes. Do not overbake or the custard will curdle. Serve the tart warm or cold, sprinkled with icing/confectioners' sugar or cinnamon. It is best eaten the day of baking.

Tarte aux Figues
FIG TART

⚜

I n the mild Breton climate, fig trees flourish. Serve these individual tarts of thinly sliced figs and crisp puff pastry warm, with crème fraîche or whipped cream.

Makes 8 individual tarts

2 lb/ 1 kg fresh figs

6 ½ oz/ 1 cup/ 200 g sugar

2 oz/ ¼ cup/ 60 g butter

Pâte feuilletée

8 oz/ 2 cups/ 250 g flour

8 oz/ 1 cup/ 250 g butter

1 tsp salt

4 fl oz/ ½ cup/ 125 ml water

METHOD
Make the pâte feuilletée dough (p.148) and chill thoroughly. Roll the dough to an 8 × 16 in/ 20 × 40 cm rectangle, trim the edges and cut into 8 equal squares. Roll each square to a very thin 4 in/ 10 cm diameter round. Prick the pastry rounds with a fork to prevent them from rising too much and chill them until firm, about 30 minutes. Heat the oven to No 7/ 425°F/ 220°C.

Cut the figs in ⅜ in/ 1 cm slices, discarding stems. Arrange the slices slightly overlapping on the pastry rounds so that they just reach the edge of the pastry. Sprinkle 2 tablespoons sugar evenly over each tart and dot the top with butter. Bake until the pastry is thoroughly browned and the surface of the figs is lightly caramelized, 20–25 minutes.

Tarte aux Oranges Confites

CANDIED ORANGE TART

⚜

SERVES 8

For candied orange slices

---

1 lb/ 500 g navel oranges

---

2 lb/ 1 kg sugar

---

1 ⅔ pint/ 1 quart/ 1 litre water

Sweet pâte brisée

---

8 oz/ 2 cups/ 250 g flour

---

4 oz/ ½ cup/ 125 g unsalted butter

---

2 egg yolks

---

2 tbsp sugar

---

1 tsp salt

3–4 tbsp cold water

---

2 eggs, beaten to mix

---

8 fl oz/ 1 cup/ 250 ml double/ heavy cream

---

11 in/ 28 cm tart tin/ pan

T he most popular and versatile Provençal sweetmeat is candied fruit. Here candied orange slices make a spectacular filling for this simple tart. Note that the slices must be candied well ahead; if you're short of time, substitute commercial candied orange strips, or even prunes.

METHOD

Cut the oranges crosswise in ¼ in/ 6 mm slices, including pith and peel. Discard the ends and any seeds. Heat the sugar with the water in a shallow pan until dissolved, then bring the syrup just to the boil. Arrange the orange slices loosely overlapping on a rack and lower it into the pan. Press a round of wax paper on top of the fruit so it is completely immersed and weigh it down with a plate.

Bring the syrup slowly to a simmer, taking 10–12 minutes. Continue poaching for another 15–18 minutes. Take the pan from the heat and let the fruit cool in the syrup. Leave it covered in the syrup at room temperature for 24 hours.

Lift out the fruit on the rack and leave it to drain for ½–1 hour. Transfer it to wax paper and leave in a cool airy place until dry, 3–5 hours. They may be stored, layered in wax paper, in an airtight container for up to a week.

Preheat the oven to No 5/ 375°F/ 190°C. Make the pâte brisée (p. 147) and chill it for 30 minutes. Roll out the dough and line the tart tin/ pan. Blind bake the shell: cut a 13 in/ 33 cm round of greaseproof paper and use it to line the shell, pressing it into the corners. Fill the shell three–quarters full with dried beans or rice to hold the dough in shape. Bake in the heated oven until the dough is set and the edges are brown, about 15 minutes. Remove the paper and beans or rice.

Whisk the eggs and cream until mixed. Arrange the orange slices overlapping in the shell and pour the cream mixture on top. Bake the tart in the heated oven until set and lightly browned, about 20 minutes. Note: if overcooked, the orange slices become tough. The tart is best served at room temperature, on the day of baking.

Tarte aux Noix

WALNUT TART

⚜

SERVES 8–10

Pâte sucrée

8 oz/ 2 cups/ 250 g flour

5 oz/ ⅔ cup/ 150 g
unsalted butter

6 egg yolks

1 tsp salt

4 oz/ 10 tbsp/ 125 g
sugar and a few drops/
½ tsp vanilla

For the filling

7 oz/ 2 cups/ 200 g
walnuts

5 oz/ ¾ cup/ 150 g light
brown sugar

2 tbsp unsalted butter,
melted

For the glaze

1 egg white, beaten until
frothy

sugar (for sprinkling)

8 in/ 20 cm tart tin/ pan
with removable base

T his walnut tart is a new twist on the little
regional mincemeat pies found in Pézenas
which, as the seat of the governor, was known as
the 'Versailles of Languedoc'. The pies are cred-
ited to the cook of Lord Clive of India, who visited
the town in 1766.

METHOD

Make the pâte sucrée (p. 149) and chill until firm,
about 30 minutes. For the filling: finely chop the
walnuts in a food processor. Add the sugar and
continue working for 1 minute. Pour in the melted butter and continue to work the mixture until
it forms coarse crumbs, 1–2 minutes longer. Without a food processor, work the nuts through the
fine blade of a grinder with the sugar. Stir in the
melted butter until it forms crumbs.

Butter the tart tin/ pan. Roll out about two-
thirds of the pastry dough and line the tin/ pan –
the dough will be quite thick. Spread the filling on
top. Roll out the remaining dough and cover the
filling, pressing the dough edges together to seal
them. Roll the rolling pin over the top of the tart
tin to cut off the excess dough. Make 2–3 holes in
the centre of the tart for steam to escape and chill
30 minutes. Heat oven to No 5/ 375°F/ 190°C.

Set the tart low down in the heated oven and
bake it 15 minutes. Turn down the heat to No 4/
350°F/ 175°C and continue baking until the tart is
crisp and brown, 25–30 minutes. Brush the top
with egg white and sprinkle generously with sugar.
Continue baking to form a crisp white glaze, about
5 minutes longer.

BREADS AND CAKES

❖

Kugelhopf aux Lardons et aux Herbes

KUGELHOPF WITH BACON AND HERBS

✣

SERVES 6–8

8 fl oz/ 1 cup/ 250 ml milk

5 oz/ ⅔ cup/ 150 g unsalted butter

1 tbsp sugar

⅔ oz/ 20 g compressed yeast, or ⅓ oz/ 10 g dry yeast

6 oz/ 1 ½ cups/ 175 g walnut halves

1 lb/ 4 cups/ 500 g flour

1 tsp salt

3 eggs

4 oz/ ½ cup/ 125 g lean smoked ham, finely chopped

1 ½ tsp dried sage

1 ½ tsp dried thyme

two 1 ⅔ pint/ 1 quart/ 1 litre kugelhopf moulds

This savoury kugelhopf, a variation on the traditional sweet raisin and nut bread, makes a welcome snack, the perfect complement to a glass of white Riesling.

METHOD

Scald the milk in a small saucepan, pour about half into a small bowl and let cool to tepid. Meanwhile add the butter and sugar to the remaining milk and continue heating, stirring until the butter is melted and the sugar dissolved, 2–3 minutes. Crumble or sprinkle the yeast over the tepid milk and leave until dissolved, about 5 minutes. Coarsely chop the walnuts, reserving 20 halves for decoration.

Sift the flour with the salt into a large bowl and make a well in the centre. Add the butter and yeast mixtures, and the eggs. With your hand, stir the central ingredients, gradually drawing in the flour to make a smooth dough. It should be very soft. Using your cupped hand, knead the dough in a slapping motion against the side of the bowl. Knead the dough until shiny and very smooth, about 5 minutes. Alternatively, mix and knead the dough in an electric mixer with a dough hook.

Transfer the dough to an oiled bowl, cover it with a damp cloth and leave to rise in a warm place until doubled in bulk, 1–1 ½ hours. Butter the kugelhopf moulds and set the reserved walnut halves in the bottom.

When risen, knead the dough lightly to knock out air and gently stir in the chopped walnuts, ham, sage and thyme. Drop the dough by spoonfuls into the moulds. Cover with a damp cloth and leave the dough to rise to the top of the mould, 30–45 minutes. Heat the oven to No 5/ 375°F/ 190°C.

Bake the kugelhopf in the heated oven until puffed and golden brown, 40–50 minutes. Turn it out on to a rack to cool. It is best eaten on the day of baking, but can be stored in an airtight container up to 3 days.

Brioche au Neufchâtel

CHEESE BRIOCHE

⚜

Makes 2 medium loaves

½ oz/ 15 g compressed yeast, or ¼ oz/ 7 g dry yeast

2 fl oz/ ¼ cup/ 60 ml lukewarm water

1 lb/ 4 cups/ 500 g unbleached flour, more if needed

1 tsp salt

1 tbsp sugar

6 eggs, beaten to mix

6 oz/175 g cheese (after the rind is removed)

6 oz/ 12 tbsp/ 175 g butter, softened

1 egg, beaten to mix with ½ teaspoon salt (for glaze)

two medium loaf tins/ pans (8 ½ × 4 ½ × 2 ½ inches/ 30 × 11 × 6 cm)

Neufchâtel is a Norman soft-paste cheese resembling Brie, and Brie or Camembert can be substituted in this brioche. Indeed it is said that the name 'brioche' comes from the use of Brie cheese rather than butter in the original recipe.

METHOD

Sprinkle or crumble the yeast over the water and let it stand for 5 minutes or until dissolved. Sift the flour on to a work surface and make a large well in the centre. Sprinkle salt and sugar on to the flour. Add the yeast mixture with the beaten eggs to the well. With your hand, gradually work in the flour to form a smooth dough; it should be quite sticky. Knead the dough on the work surface, lifting it up and throwing it down until it is very elastic and resembles chamois leather, about 5 minutes. Work in more flour if necessary so that at the end of kneading, the dough is sticky but holds together in one piece.

Transfer the dough to an oiled bowl, turn it over so the top is oiled and cover the bowl with a damp cloth. Leave it in a warm place for an hour or until doubled in bulk. Butter the loaf tins/pans, line them with greaseproof/wax paper and butter the paper. Cut the cheese into cubes; if necessary leave at room temperature to soften.

Knead the dough lightly to knock out air. Work in the softened cheese and butter, squeezing with your fist until it is completely incorporated. Divide the dough in half and shape it into two loaves. Set the loaves in the prepared tins/pans, cover with a cloth and let them rise in a warm place for

½–1 hour, or until the tins/pans are almost full. Heat the oven to No 6/ 400°F/ 200°C.

Brush the loaves with egg glaze and score the tops with a sharp knife. Bake in the heated oven for 45–55 minutes or until the loaves start to shrink away from the sides of the pan and sound hollow when tapped on the bottom. Unmould and cool them on a rack. Cheese brioche is best eaten the day of baking, but day-old brioche also toasts well.

Le Floron

THREE-GRAIN BREAD

⚜

Makes 2 large loaves

½ oz/ 15 g compressed yeast, or ¼ oz/ 7 g dry yeast

16 fl oz/ 2 cups/ 500 ml lukewarm water

1 lb/ 4 cups/ 500 g plain/ all-purpose flour, more as needed

3 oz/ ⅔ cup/ 90 g rye flour

3 ¼ oz/ ¾ cup/ 100 g buckwheat flour

1 tbsp salt

1 egg yolk mixed with 1 tbsp water, for glaze

T his loaf is typical of the multi-grain breads favoured by Breton bakers – in the old days wheat was scarce in Brittany but buckwheat prospered. In French, buckwheat is called 'sarrasin' because supposedly it was introduced to Europe by the Saracens who invaded in the 14th century, pushing north as far as the Loire.

METHOD

Crumble or sprinkle the yeast over 6–8 tablespoonfuls of the lukewarm water in a small bowl. Let stand until dissolved, about 5 minutes. Sift the flours and salt into a large, wide bowl, make a well in the centre and add the remaining water and the dissolved yeast. With your hand mix some of the flour with the water, drawing in enough flour to make a thick batter. Sprinkle more of the flour on top of the batter, cover and leave in a warm place until bubbles break the surface, 30–40 minutes.

Mix the batter with the remaining flour to make a smooth dough. It will be very sticky. Turn the dough on to a floured work surface and work in more flour until the dough no longer sticks to your fingers. Knead it until it is smooth and elastic, 5–8 minutes. Alternatively, knead the dough in an electric mixer with the dough hook.

Transfer the dough to an oiled bowl, turn it over so the top is oiled and cover the bowl with a damp cloth. Leave in a warm place to rise until doubled in bulk, 1–1 ½ hours. Butter the baking sheet.

Punch the air out of the dough. Divide it in half and on a floured board shape each half into a loose round ball. Fold the edges to the centre, turning to make a tight round ball. Flip the balls so the smooth side is uppermost and set them on the prepared baking sheet. Cover with a cloth and let them rise in a warm place until almost doubled, about 45 minutes. Cut a flexible stencil of card in the shape of a fleur-de-lys.

Heat the oven to No 6/ 400°F/ 200°C. Set the stencil on a loaf, thickly sift flour over the loaf and then carefully remove the stencil using a knife or metal spatula. With a small paint brush or the point of a teaspoon, glaze the 'ermine' shape left on the loaf with the egg yolk and water mixture. With the point of a very sharp knife, slash a continuous circle around the bread, about 1 in/ 2.5 cm above the edge of the baking sheet. Repeat with the second loaf.

Bake the loaves in the heated oven for 15 minutes. Lower the heat to No 4/ 350°F/ 175°C and continue baking until the loaves are brown and sound hollow when tapping on the bottom, 30–40 minutes longer. They are best eaten the day of baking and they freeze well.

Gochtiale

DEMI BRIOCHE

Makes 2 medium loaves

½ oz/ 15 g compressed
yeast, or ¼ oz/ 7 g dry
yeast

4 fl oz/ ½ cup/ 125 ml
lukewarm milk

9 oz/ 2 ½ cups/ 300 g
unbleached flour, more
if needed

2 oz/ ⅓ cup/ 60 g sugar.

½ tsp salt

2 eggs, beaten to mix

3 ¼ oz/ 7 tbsp/ 100 g
salted butter

1 egg beaten with ½ tsp
salt (for glaze)

a 7 in/ 18 cm round cake
tin/ pan

T his 'gochtiale' from Brittany has a pleasant-
ly light texture, with less butter and eggs
than a classic brioche. With its high sugar content,
it toasts well.

METHOD

Crumble or sprinkle the yeast over the milk and let
it stand for 5 minutes or until dissolved. Sift the
flour on to a work surface and make a large well in
the centre. Sprinkle the sugar and salt on to the
flour. Add the yeast mixture with the beaten eggs
to the well. With your hand, gradually work in
the flour to form a smooth dough; it should be
quite sticky. Knead the dough on the work surface,
lifting it up and throwing it down until it is very
elastic and resembles chamois leather, about 10
minutes. Work in more flour if necessary so that
at the end of kneading, the dough is slightly sticky
but peels easily from the work surface.

Transfer the dough to an oiled bowl, turn it over
so the top is oiled and cover the bowl with a damp
cloth. Leave it in a warm place for an hour or until
doubled in bulk. Butter the cake tin/ pan.

Work the dough lightly to knock out air.
Squeeze the butter with your fist until it is pliable. Add it to the dough and knead, squeezing
with your fist and throwing it down, until the butter is completely incorporated, 5–10 minutes. If you
like, the dough can be kneaded and the butter
added using an electric mixer with the dough
hook.

On a floured board shape the dough into a
ball, folding the edges to the centre. Flip the ball

so the smooth side is upwards and drop gently into the prepared pan. Cover with a cloth and let rise in a warm place until the dough is almost doubled, ½–1 hour. Heat the oven to No 5/ 375°F/ 190°C.

Brush the brioche with the egg yolk mixture. With the point of a very sharp knife, slash a cross on the top of the loaf. Bake the brioche in the heated oven until the loaf starts to shrink away from the sides of the pan and sounds hollow when tapped on the bottom, 40–50 minutes. Unmould and cool on a rack. Brioche is best eaten the day of baking and it freezes well.

Christstollen

CHRISTMAS FRUIT BREAD

⚜

Makes 1 medium loaf

3 ½ oz/ ¾ cup/ 100 g raisins

1 ¾ oz/ ½ cup/ 50 g candied orange peel, finely chopped

¾ oz/ ¼ cup/ 25 g candied cherries, chopped

grated zest of 1 orange

3 tbsp rum

8 fl oz/ 1 cup/ 250 ml milk

½ oz/ 15 g compressed yeast, or ¼ oz/ 7 g dry yeast

12 oz/ 3 cups/ 375 g flour, more if needed

1 ½ oz/ ¼ cup/ 50 g sugar

¾ tsp salt

1 egg, beaten to mix

2 oz/ ¼ cup/ 60 g unsalted butter, melted

3 oz/ ½ cup/ 75 g blanched almonds, finely chopped

Christstollen, the pride of Alsace, is delicious toasted, and because of its high fruit content it keeps so well that one old book advises hiding away a slice or two until Easter.

METHOD

Macerate the raisins, candied fruits and orange zest in the rum until well saturated, 1–2 hours. Butter a baking sheet.

Scald the milk and let it cool to tepid. Crumble or sprinkle the yeast on top and leave until dissolved, about 5 minutes. Sift the flour with the sugar and salt on to a work surface and form a well in the centre. Put in the yeast mixture with the egg and melted butter. Mix with your fingers, slowly drawing in the flour to form a dough; it should be soft but not sticky – if necessary, add more flour. Sprinkle the work surface with flour and knead the dough until very smooth and elastic, about 5 minutes. Alternatively mix and knead the dough in an electric mixer with the dough hook.

Press the dough flat, sprinkle it with the fruits and almonds and roll it into a cylinder. Knead the dough again until the fruits are evenly distributed, about 1 minute. Shape the dough into a ball, transfer it to an oiled bowl, and flip so the top is oiled. Cover the bowl with a damp cloth and leave in a warm place until the dough is well risen and almost doubled in bulk, 1 ½–2 hours.

Knead the dough lightly to knock out the air. Shape it into a ball on a floured work surface, then press out with your fist to an oval. With the rolling pin, roll one end of the oval flatter than the other. Fold the thick side on to the flatter one and press the top to seal the layers. Set the bread on the prepared baking sheet, cover with a cloth and leave in a warm place to rise until well puffed. Heat the oven to No 6/ 400°F/ 200°C.

Bake the bread in the heated oven for 15 minutes, then turn the oven down to No 2/ 300°F/ 150°C and continue baking until browned and the bottom sounds hollow when tapped with your fist, 25–35 minutes longer. Transfer it to a rack. While still hot, brush the top with melted butter and sprinkle thickly with icing/ confectioners's sugar.

For the coating

3 tbsp unsalted butter, melted

8 oz/ 1 ¼ cups/ 250 g icing/ confectioners' sugar

Fouace

FLAT YEAST BREAD

Makes 1 flat loaf to serve 4

⅓ oz/ 10 g compressed yeast, or ⅙ oz/ 5 g dry yeast

4 fl oz/ ½ cup/ 125 ml lukewarm milk

10 oz/ 2 ½ cups/ 300 g flour, more if needed

2 eggs

1 tsp salt

2 tsp sugar

4 tbsp finely chopped candied lemon peel, or stoned/ pitted black olives, or 2 tbsp chopped fresh thyme, oregano or rosemary

2 ½ oz/ ⅓ cup/ 75 g unsalted butter

1 egg, beaten with ½ tsp salt (for glaze)

T his Provençal bread is high in yeast, so it rises quickly, forming a flat, oval loaf. Slashed to resemble a giant leaf, 'fouace' is best eaten warm, broken into pieces at the table.

METHOD

In a small bowl, crumble or sprinkle the yeast over 3–4 tablespoons of the milk. Mix in enough of the flour to make a soft, sticky dough and let this starter rise in a warm place for 15–20 minutes. Sift the remaining flour on a board or marble slab and make a large well in the centre. Add the yeast starter, eggs, salt, sugar, candied lemon peel or other flavouring, and the remaining milk. Briefly mix the centre ingredients, then gradually draw in the flour to form a dough. Knead the dough into a ball; it should be soft but not sticky.

Knead the dough by lifting it up and slapping it on the work surface for 5–10 minutes until very elastic. Pound the butter to soften it, then work it into the dough, kneading to incorporate the butter thoroughly. Transfer the dough to a lightly floured bowl, cover and let rise at room temperature for 1 hour or until nearly doubled in bulk.

Transfer the risen dough to a floured board or marble slab, patting to knock out the air. Roll the dough into an oval about ¾ in/ 2 cm thick on a lightly floured baking sheet. Slit it diagonally like the veins on a leaf, pulling the slits apart with your fingers. Let the dough rise until nearly doubled, 15–25 minutes. Preheat the oven to No 6/ 400°F/ 200°C. Brush the bread with the egg glaze and bake until golden brown, 10–12 minutes.

Gâteau au Chocolat de Fernand Point

FERNAND POINT'S CHOCOLATE CAKE

⚜

A mong the more feasible of Lyon's chocolate treats is this gâteau of the legendary Fernand Point, father of modern cooking, whose restaurant flourished in Vienne south of Lyon. It is delicious served with a coffee custard sauce (p. 151).

(p. 151)

METHOD

Preheat the oven to No 4/ 350°F/ 175°C. Butter the cake tin/ pan, line the base with a round of grease-proof/ wax paper and butter the paper. Sprinkle the tin/ pan with flour, discarding the excess. Work the chocolate in a food processor, finely chop it with a knife, or coarsely grate it. Note: the texture should be slightly granular. Sift the flour.

Warm the butter over a pan of hot water until it is soft enough to pour. Do not let it melt to oil. Let it cool slightly. Beat the egg yolks with the sugar until thick and the mixture leaves a ribbon trail when the whisk is lifted, about 5 minutes. Stiffly whip the egg whites separately.

Beat the butter into the egg yolk mixture, followed by the chocolate and then the flour, using an electric mixer if you like. With a spatula, fold in the egg whites in three batches. Pour the batter into the prepared tin/pan and bake in the heated oven 35–45 minutes until the cake shrinks slightly from the sides of the pan and the top springs back when lightly pressed with a fingertip.

Run a knife around the edge of the cake and turn it out on a rack to cool. It is best eaten the day of baking, but can be stored 2–3 days in an airtight container. For serving, sprinkle it generously with powdered cocoa or icing/confectioners' sugar.

SERVES 6–8

4 oz/ 125 g dessert/ semisweet chocolate

4 oz/ 1 cup/ 125 g flour

4 oz/ ½ cup/ 125 g unsalted butter

4 eggs, separated

5 oz/ ¾ cup/ 150 g sugar

powdered cocoa or icing/ confectioners' sugar (for sprinkling)

9 in/ 22 cm straight-sided cake tin/ pan or springform cake tin/ pan

Pain d'Épices

HONEY SPICE BREAD

⚜

**Makes two medium
loaves to serve 10–12**

½ pint/ 1 ¼ cups/
300 ml milk

6 ½ oz/ 1 cup/ 200 g
sugar

1 lb/1 ½ cups/ 500 g
honey

12 oz/3 cups/ 375 g rye
flour

6 ½ oz/ 1 ⅔ cups/ 200 g
plain flour

2 eggs yolks

1 oz/ 2 tbsp/ 30 g
chopped, candied
orange peel

2 tsp baking soda

½ tsp ground anise

½ tsp ground cinnamon

½ tsp ground cloves

For the icing

1 egg white

3 oz/ ⅔ cup/ 90 g icing/
confectioners' sugar

two 10 × 4 × 3 in/
25 × 10 × 7.5 cm loaf
pans/ tins

'Pain d'épices', a Burgundian speciality, is akin to English gingerbread, but anise predominates in the blend of spices and much more honey is added. Be sure to keep the bread at least 3 days before you try it, so the flavours mellow.

METHOD

Heat the milk, sugar and honey in a saucepan, stirring until the sugar dissolves. Bring just to the boil, then remove from the heat and cool to tepid. Stir the two flours together in a bowl, make a well in the centre and add three-quarters of the cooled honey mixture and the egg yolks. Stir with a wooden spoon, gradually drawing in the flour to make a smooth batter. In a small bowl, mix the candied peel, baking soda and spices. Stir in the remaining honey mixture and stir this mixture into flour batter. Cover and refrigerate 8 hours.

Preheat the oven to No 3/ 325°F/ 160°C. Butter the loaf pans/ tins, line them with greaseproof/ wax paper and butter the paper. Spoon the batter into the pans/ tins and bake in the oven until a skewer inserted 2 in/ 5 cm from the end of the mould comes out clean, 1–1 ½ hours. Note: spice bread should be slightly underbaked, so it is soft in the centre and has not started to shrink from the sides of the pan. Let the breads cool until tepid, then turn on to a rack, removing the paper.

While the loaves are still warm, make the icing. Whisk the egg white until frothy. Gradually whisk in the icing/ confectioners' sugar to make an icing that pours easily. Pour it over the warm breads so it thinly coats the top and drips down the sides.

Michel Helias' Gâteau Breton

MICHEL HELIAS' BUTTER CAKE

⚜

Once a week, Breton pâtissier Michel Helias bakes gâteau Breton, a golden crusty version of pound cake that highlights good butter. Gâteaux Bretons are common, recognizable by their latticed tops, but the Helias version flavoured with rum is undeniably superior.

METHOD

Heat the oven to No 3/ 325°F/ 160°C. Thoroughly butter the tart tin/ pan. Set aside a tablespoonful of the egg yolks for glaze.

Sift the flour on to a work surface and make a large well in the centre. Cut the butter in small pieces and put it in the well with the sugar, egg yolks and rum. Work them together with your fingertips until smooth. Gradually incorporate the flour using the fingers and heel of your hand in a rocking motion, and then work the dough gently until smooth. It will be sticky at this point and must be mixed with the help of a pastry scraper or metal spatula.

Transfer the dough to the buttered tin/ pan or individual tins/ pans and smooth it with your fist to an even layer, wetting the back of your hand to prevent sticking. Brush the surface of the dough with the reserved egg yolk and mark a lattice design with the prongs of a fork.

Bake in the oven for 1–1 ¼ hours (35–45 minutes for smaller cakes) until the top is golden and firm to the touch. The inside should remain moist. Leave to cool, then unmould the cake or cakes carefully on to a rack. Gâteau Breton can be stored for up to a week in an airtight container.

Makes 1 cake to serve 6 or about 6 individual cakes

6 egg yolks

9 oz/ 2 ¼ cups/ 275 g flour

8 oz/ 1 cup/ 250 g salted butter

6 ½ oz/ 1 cup/ 200 g sugar

1 fl oz/ 2 tbsp/ 30 ml rum

One 8 in/ 21 cm tart tin/ pan or six 4 in/10 cm tartlet tins/ pans

Gâteau Frangipane

ALMOND SPONGE CAKE

⚜

SERVES 4

8 oz/ 2 cups/ 250 g
ground blanched
almonds

6 ½ oz/ 1 cup/ 200 g
sugar

4 eggs

2 egg whites

5 oz/ ⅔ cup/ 150 g
unsalted butter, melted

2 tbsp cornflour/ starch

1 tsp orange flower
water, or few drops/
½ tsp vanilla

For the icing

5 oz/ 1 ½ cups/ 150 g
icing/ confectioners'
sugar, more if needed

3 tbsp ratafia, or 3 tbsp
water with a few drops/
½ tsp vanilla

9 in/ 23 cm springform
pan or straight–sided
cake tin/ pan

Deliciously moist, this cake may be topped with a simple dusting of powdered sugar, or with glacé icing flavoured with ratafia. When the ratafia is based on red grape juice, the icing shades to a dusty designer pink.

METHOD

Preheat the oven to No 3/ 3250°F/ 160°C. Butter the cake tin/ pan, line it with a round of grease-proof/ wax paper and butter the paper.

In a food processor, work the almonds with the sugar until mixed. With motor running, add the whole eggs, one by one, then the egg whites. Work for 5 minutes, then transfer the batter to a bowl. Fold in the melted butter with a wooden spatula, then fold in the cornflour/ starch and orange flower water or vanilla.

Pour the batter into the prepared pan and bake in the heated oven 40–45 minutes until the cake is firm to the touch in the centre and shrinks slightly from the sides of the pan. Transfer it to a rack to cool. The cake can be stored in an airtight container up to a week.

For the icing: sift the sugar into a small bowl and stir in the ratafia or water and vanilla. Heat the bowl in a water bath (p. 152) until the icing is tepid. It should coat the back of a spoon. If too thick add a little more liquid; if too thin beat in more sifted sugar. Set the cooled cake on a rack, pour over the icing and spread it quickly with a palette knife so it drips down the sides. Leave it to cool and set, then transfer it to a serving plate.

Croquants

ALMOND COOKIES

✣

T hese meringue-based cookies bake to be very firm, and are designed to be dipped in a glass of wine and soaked for a few seconds before eating. They should be thoroughly baked so the almonds develop a toasted flavour.

METHOD

Coarsely mince/grind the almonds in a food processor, or chop them with a knife. Whisk the egg whites until frothy and gradually beat in the sugar. Continue whisking until a thick meringue mixture is formed, 2–3 minutes. Note: it will be soft, not stiff. Add the almond extract. Using a wooden spoon, stir in the flour and almonds. Note: do not overwork it or the croquants will be tough. Refrigerate the dough for 30 minutes.

Butter and flour a baking sheet. On a well floured surface press down the dough to ⅜ in/ 1 cm thickness using your hand. Cut into ¾ in/ 2 cm x 3 in/ 7.5 cm bars and set them on the prepared baking sheet, leaving room to spread slightly. Refrigerate until very firm, at least an hour.

Heat the oven to No 7/ 425°F/ 220°C. Brush the croquants with the glaze and bake them near the top of the oven until firm and brown, 8–12 minutes. Let them cool slightly, then transfer to a rack to cool completely. Leave them to dry in the open air for 12 hours before storing in an airtight container for up to 1 month.

Makes 3 dozen

4 oz/ ⅔ cup/ 125 g blanched almonds

2 egg whites

8 oz/ 1¼ cups/ 250 g sugar

½ tsp almond extract

4 oz/ 1 cup/ 125 g flour

1 egg, beaten to mix with ½ tsp salt (for glaze)

Leckerli

HAZELNUT GINGERBREAD COOKIES

⚜

Makes 3 dozen bars

5 oz/ 1 cup/ 150 g
shelled hazelnuts

10 oz/ 2 ½ cups/ 300 g
flour

3 tbsp baking powder

½ tsp ground cinnamon

½ tsp ground cloves

pinch of anise, crushed

pinch ground cardamom

pinch of salt

3 oz/ ⅓ cup/ 175 g
honey

3 oz/ 6 tbsp/ 90 g
unsalted butter

2 tbsp fresh lemon juice

2 tbsp candied orange
peel, chopped

2 eggs, beaten to mix

For the icing

1 egg white

4 ½ oz/ 1 cup/ 135 g
icing/ confectioners'
sugar, more if needed

11 × 17 in/28 × 44 cm
shallow baking tin/pan

I find regular gingerbread recipes a bit dry, but the following hazelnut version is superb.

METHOD

Butter the tin/ pan, line the bottom with grease-proof/ wax paper and butter the paper. Heat the oven to No 5/ 375°F/ 190°C. Toast the hazelnuts on a baking sheet until brown, 12–15 minutes. Let cool slightly, then rub them if necessary in a coarse cloth to remove the skins. Then chop the nuts finely by hand or in a food processor.

Sift the flour with the baking powder, cinnamon, cloves, anise, cardamom and salt. In a saucepan, heat the honey, sugar and butter, stirring until the sugar is dissolved and the butter melted. Take from the heat, mix in the lemon juice and candied orange peel, and let cool. Beat in half of the flour mixture and the chopped nuts, add the eggs, and then beat in the remaining flour. Beat for 2 minutes until the dough is smooth, pliable and still slightly sticky. Alternatively, beat with the dough hook of an electric mixer.

Spread the dough in the prepared tin/ pan in an even layer about ⅜ in/ 1 cm thick. Bake until it is golden brown and still soft, about 20 minutes. Note: do not overbake or the leckerli will be dry.

A few minutes before the dough is cooked, whisk the egg white until frothy, add the icing/confectioners' sugar and whisk until smooth; the icing should pour easily but if it is thin, add more sugar. As soon as the cookies are done, brush on a light coating of icing. Allow to cool for 5 minutes, then cut into bars, discarding the dry edges.

SOME BASICS OF FRENCH COOKING

⚜

ARROWROOT

Arrowroot (or potato starch) is used to thicken sauces lightly at the end of cooking. Mix the arrowroot in a cup with water, allowing about 1 tablespoon of water per teaspoon of arrowroot. It will make a thin, opaque mixture, which separates on standing but can easily be recombined. Whisk this mixture into a boiling liquid, adding just enough to thicken the sauce to the desired consistency. Do not boil the sauce for more than 2–3 minutes or it may become thin again.

BARDING FAT

Barding fat is thinly sliced pork fat available at most butchers. Barding fat is often wrapped around meat when it has little or no natural fat. It is also used for lining terrine moulds, where it is important to enclose meat to maintain a consistent level of moisture.

BLANCHING

Blanching is a preliminary to cooking. Generally, the food is put in cold unsalted water, brought slowly to the boil, skimmed, and then simmered for 3–5 minutes. Green vegetables, however, are blanched in water that is already boiling. The term 'to blanch' is misleading, for as well as whitening, it removes salt and other strong flavours, notably from bacon; it firms meats like sweetbreads and brains; it sets the brilliant colour of green vegetables and herbs, which often do not need further cooking; it loosens the skins of nuts and fruits like almonds and tomatoes; and it rids rice and potatoes of excess starch.

BLIND BAKING

Pastry shells are blind baked (empty) before the filling is added. This procedure is used if the filling is not to be cooked in the shell, or if the filling is especially moist and might soak the pastry during baking. The dried beans or rice for blind baking can be kept and re-used.

FOR PIES

Heat the oven to 400°F/ 200°C/ No 6. Crumple a round of parchment paper and line the chilled pastry shell, pressing the paper well into the corners; fill the shell with dried beans or rice. Bake the pastry in the oven for 15 minutes or until the edges are set and lightly browned. Remove the paper and beans or rice and continue baking until the base is firm and dry, for 4–5 minutes if the pie is to be baked again with the filling, or until well browned, 8–10 minutes, to bake the shell completely.

FOR TARTELETTES

Heat the oven to 400°F/ 200°C/ No 6. Line the chilled pastry shells with a round of crumpled parchment paper and fill with dried beans or rice. Alternatively, put a smaller tartelette pan inside each shell. Set the pans on a baking sheet and bake in the oven for 8–10 minutes. Remove the paper and beans or rice and continue baking until the pastry is firm and lightly browned, for 3–4 minutes if the tartelettes are to be baked again with the filling, or until well browned, 5–7 minutes, to bake the tartelettes completely.

BOUQUET GARNI

A bundle of aromatic herbs used for flavouring braisés, ragoûts and sauces. It should include a sprig of thyme, a bay leaf and several sprigs of parsley, tied together with string. Green leek and celery tops may also be included.

BROWN STOCK

See Stock, brown.

CÈPES

See Wild mushrooms, to clean.

CHESTNUTS
TO PEEL

With a small knife make a slit at the end of each nut. Put them in a pan of cold water and bring just to the boil. Use a slotted spoon to lift out a few nuts at a time and peel them while still hot, removing both the thick outer skin and the thin inner skin. If the chestnuts cool and become difficult to peel, quickly reheat them. Do not allow them to heat too long, or the chestnuts will become soft and fall apart.

CHICKEN
See Cutting up a raw bird.

TO CUT UP

CHICKEN STOCK
See Stock, chicken.

CRÈME CHANTILLY
For ingredient measurements, see individual recipes. Put the chilled cream in a bowl over ice and water and whisk until stiff. Note: if the cream is not cold it may curdle before it stiffens. Add sugar to taste, with vanilla or other flavouring, and continue whisking until the cream stiffens again. Note: do not over-beat or the cream will curdle. Crème Chantilly can be stored in the refrigerator for up to 12 hours. It will separate slightly on standing, but will recombine if stirred.

CRÈME FRAÎCHE
This French cream has a slightly tart flavour which is particularly good in sauces. To make 1 ¼ pints/ 3 cups/ 750 ml of crème fraîche, stir together in a saucepan 16 fl oz/ 2 cups/ 500 ml double/ heavy cream and 8 fl oz/ 1 cup/ 250 ml buttermilk or sour cream. Heat gently until just below body temperature (25°C/ 75°F). Pour the cream into a container and partly cover it. Keep it at this temperature for 6–8 hours or until it has thickened and tastes slightly acid. The cream will thicken faster on a hot day. Stir it and store it in the refrigerator; it will keep for up to 2 weeks.

CROÛTES
Croûtes are fried or toasted slices of bread used to add texture or to garnish dishes. If using French bread, cut the loaf into the thin diagonal slices; if using sliced white bread, cut the bread in squares,

triangles, rounds or hearts, discarded the crusts.

FOR TOASTED CROÛTES

Bake the sliced bread in an oven heated to 350°F/175°C/No 4 for 10–15 minutes, turning the croûtes halfway through so they brown evenly on both sides. For a lightly fried effect, brush the sliced bread on both sides with melted butter before baking.

FOR FRIED CROÛTES

Heat enough oil or butter, or a combination of the two, in a frying pan to coat the bottom generously. Add the slices of bread in a single layer, brown them on both sides over a brisk heat and drain them on paper towels.

CROÛTONS

Cut sliced white bread in cubes, discarding crusts. Fry as for croûtes, using enough fat for the croûtons to float. Stir briskly so they brown evenly.

CUTTING UP A RAW BIRD

With a sharp knife, cut between leg and body, following the outline of the thigh until the leg joint is visible. Locate the 'oyster' piece of meat lying against the backbone, and cut around it so it remains attached to the thigh. Twist the leg sharply outwards to break the thigh joint. Cut forwards to detach each leg from the body, including the oyster meat. With a knife or poultry shears, cut away and remove the backbone. Cut along the breastbone to halve the carcass. Cut off the wingtips. The bird is now in 4 pieces.

To cut in 8 pieces, divide each breast in half, cutting diagonally through the meat, then through the breast and rib bones so a portion of breast meat is cut off with the wing. Trim the rib bones. Then, cut the legs in half through the joint, using the white line of fat on the underside as a guide. Trim the drumsticks and any protruding bones with poultry shears.

DEGLAZE

To deglaze a pan, boil the juices to a glaze (see separate entry) that sticks to the bottom of the pan (this may happen naturally during cooking). Pour off any fat, add liquid and boil, stirring to dissolve the glaze. Continue boiling until the liquid is reduced and has plenty of flavour.

DUCK
To cut up

See Cutting up a raw bird.

EGGS
To poach

Bring a large shallow pan of water to a rolling boil. Add 3 tablespoons vinegar per 1 ⅔ pints/ 1 quart/ 1 litre water. Break up to four eggs, one by one, into places where the liquid bubbles. Lower the heat and poach the eggs for 3–4 minutes until the yolk is fairly firm but still soft to the touch. Gently lift out the eggs with a slotted spoon and drain on paper towels. Trim the stringy edges with a pair of scissors. If the poached eggs are not to be used immediately, transfer them to a bowl of cold water. The eggs can then be reheated just before serving by soaking them in a bowl of hot water for 2 minutes and draining them.

FISH STOCK

See Stock, fish.

FLAMING

Food is flamed in spirit or in fortified wine with a high alcohol content. After flaming, only the essence remains and food is slightly toasted. To flame: heat the alcohol in a small pan, light it and pour over the hot food. Continue basting with liquid until the flame goes out. If the dish contains sugar, cooking should be continued until the sugar caramelizes.

GLAZE
To reduce to a

When the cooking juices of meat or poultry are boiled down, they darken and caramelize to a shiny glaze which gives rich flavour to sauces and gravies. Glaze should be deep golden and of a sticky consistency. If cooked too far, it will burn.

JULIENNE STRIPS

Julienne strips are matchstick length but more

finely cut. For root vegetables, trim the sides of the vegetable to a square, then slice into 2 in/ 5 cm lengths. Cut the lengths in thin vertical slices. Stack the slices and cut in thin strips. For celery, green pepper and similar vegetables, cut lengthwise in thin 2 in/ 5 cm strips.

KNEADED BUTTER

Kneaded butter is a paste made with butter and flour that is used to thicken a liquid at the end of cooking. It makes a richer, more traditional sauce than a starch thickener such as arrowroot. To make the kneaded butter, mash equal amounts of butter and flour together with your fingers or a fork until smooth. Add the kneaded butter gradually to boiling liquid, whisking constantly so that the butter melts and distributes the flour, thus thickening the sauce evenly. Continue boiling, adding the butter piece by piece until the sauce has thickened to the desired consistency. Kneaded butter can be made in large quantities and kept for several weeks in the refrigerator.

LARDONS

Lardons are usually cut from bacon, but other fatty cuts of pork can also be used. To cut the lardons, trim the rind from the bacon and slice it ¼ in/ 6 mm thick, then cut across the slices into short strips.

MOREL MUSHROOMS
TO CLEAN

See Wild mushrooms, to clean.

MUSSELS
TO CLEAN

Wash the mussels under cold running water, scraping the shells clean with a knife and removing any weeds. Discard any shells which do not close when tapped, because this indicates that the mussel may be dead. The 'beard', or tough string dangling from inside the shell, should be removed only just before cooking the mussels.

For ingredient measurements, see individual recipes. Sift flour onto a work surface and make a large well in the centre. Pound the butter with a rolling pin to soften it. Put the butter, eggs or egg yolks, salt and water in the well with flavourings such as sugar. Work together with your fingertips until partly mixed. Gradually draw in the flour with a pastry scraper or metal spatula, pulling the dough into large crumbs using the fingertips of both hands. If the crumbs are dry, sprinkle with another tablespoon of water. Press the dough together: it should be soft but not sticky. Work small portions of dough, pushing away from you on the work surface with the heel of your hand, then gathering it up with a scraper. Continue until the dough is smooth and pliable. Press the dough into a ball, wrap it and chill it for 30 minutes or until firm. Pâte brisée can be refrigerated overnight, or frozen.

PASTRY DOUGHS
PÂTE BRISÉE

For ingredient measurements, see individual recipes. Cut the butter into pieces. In a small saucepan, gently heat the water, salt and butter until the butter is melted. Meanwhile, sift the flour on to a piece of paper. Bring the butter mixture just to the boil (prolonged boiling evaporates the water and changes the proportions of the dough). Remove from the heat and immediately add all the flour. Beat vigorously with a wooden spoon for a few moments until the mixture pulls away from the sides of the pan to form a ball. Beat for ½ –1 minute over a low heat to dry the dough. Beat one egg until mixed and set it aside. Beat the remaining eggs into the dough, one at a time, and beat thoroughly after each addition. Beat in enough of the reserved egg so that the dough is shiny and just falls from the spoon. If too much egg is added, the dough will be too soft and not hold its shape.

PÂTE À CHOUX

PÂTE FEUILLETÉE

For ingredient measurements, see individual recipes. Melt or soften 1 tablespoon of the butter. Keep the rest of the butter cold. Sift the flour on to a cold marble slab or board, make a well in the centre and add the salt, water and the 1 tablespoon of butter. Work together with your fingertips until well mixed, then gradually work in the flour. If the dough is dry, add more water to form a soft but not sticky dough. Note: do not overwork the dough or it will become elastic. Press the dough into a ball, wrap it and chill it 15 minutes. Lightly flour the butter, put it between two sheets of greaseproof wax paper and flatten it with a rolling pin. Fold it, replace between the paper and continue pounding and folding it until pliable but not sticky; it should be the same consistency as the dough. Shape the butter into a 6 in/ 15 cm square and flour it lightly.

Roll out the dough on a floured marble slab or board to a 12 in/ 30 cm square, thicker in the centre than at the sides. Set the butter in the centre and fold the dough around it like an envelope.

Make sure the working surface is well floured. Place the dough seam-side down and lightly pound it with a rolling pin to flatten it slightly. Roll it out to a rectangle about 7 in/ 18 cm wide and 20 in/ 50 cm long. Fold the rectangle into three, like a business letter. Seal the edges with the rolling pin and turn the dough a quarter turn (90°) to bring the closed seam to your left side so the dough opens like a book. This is called a turn. Roll out again and fold in three. Wrap the dough and chill 15 minutes.

Repeat the rolling process until you have rolled and folded the dough 6 times, with a 15 minute rest in the refrigerator between every 2 turns. Chill the puff pastry at least 15 minutes before using it.

PÂTE À PÂTÉ

Follow the steps for making pâte brisée, adding the lard or butter and oil to the well with the eggs.

For ingredient measurements, see individual recipes. Sift the flour on to a work surface and make a large well in the centre. (Note: in nut pastries, ground walnuts or hazelnuts may replace some of the flour.) Pound the butter with a rolling pin to soften. Put the butter, egg yolks, salt, sugar and vanilla into the well and work with your fingertips until they are well mixed and then the sugar is partly dissolved. Draw in the flour, then work the dough and chill as when making Pâte brisée.

PÂTE SUCRÉE

See Arrowroot.

POTATO STARCH

Trim and discard flaps of skin, tips of forelegs and any excess bone. Using a heavy knife or cleaver, divide the rabbit crosswise into three sections: back legs, back, and forelegs including rib cage. Cut between the back legs to separate them; trim the end of backbone. Chop the front of the rabbit in 2 to separate forelegs. Cut the back crosswise into 2 or 3 pieces, depending on size, giving 6 or 7 pieces. Leave the kidneys attached to the ribs. For 8 or 9 pieces, cut each leg in two crosswise.

RABBIT
TO CUT IN PIECES

Discard the stems from the spinach and wash the leaves well in several changes of water. Pack the wet leaves in a pan, cover and cook over medium heat, stirring once, until the leaves are wilted, about 5 minutes. Drain the spinach and leave to cool. Squeeze it by handfuls to extract as much water as possible.

SPINACH
PREPARING AND
COOKING

For about 4 pints/ 2 ½ quarts/ 2.5 litres stock, roast 5 lb/ 2.3 kg veal bones (you may use half veal bones and half beef bones, if you like) in a very hot oven for 20 minutes. Add 2 quartered carrots and 2 quartered onions and continue roasting until very brown, about 30 minutes longer. Trans-

STOCK, BROWN

fer the bones and vegetables to a stock pot, discarding any fat. Add a bouquet garni (see separate entry), 1 teaspoon whole peppercorns, 1 tablespoon tomato purée/paste and about 4 quarts/ 5 quarts/ 5 litres water. Bring slowly to the boil, then simmer uncovered for 4–5 hours, skimming occasionally. Strain the stock, taste and, if the flavour is not concentrated, boil it until well reduced. Chill the stock and skim off any fat before using. Stock can be refrigerated for up to 3 days, or frozen.

STOCK, CHICKEN

Duck and other poultry bones can be substituted for the chicken. For about 4 pints/ 2 ½ quarts/ 2.5 litres of stock, in a large pan combine 3 lb/ 1.4 kg chicken backs, necks and bones; 1 onion, quartered; 1 carrot, quartered; 1 stalk celery, cut into pieces; a bouquet garni (see separate entry); 1 teaspoon peppercorns and about 6 ½ pints/ 4 quarts/ 4 litres water. Bring slowly to the boil, skimming often. Simmer uncovered, skimming occasionally, for 2–3 hours. Strain, taste, and if the stock is not concentrated, boil it until well reduced. Refrigerate it and, before using, skim any solidified fat from the surface. Stock can be kept for up to 3 days in the refrigerator, or frozen.

STOCK, FISH

For about 1 ⅔ pints/ 1 quart/ 1 litre stock, break 1 ½ lb/ 750 g fish bones into pieces and wash them thoroughly. In a pan cook 1 sliced onion in 1 tablespoon butter until soft but not brown. Add the fish bones, 1 ⅔ pints/ 1 quart/ 1 litre water, a bouquet garni (see separate entry), 10 peppercorns and 8 fl oz/ 1 cup/ 250 ml dry white wine. Bring to the boil and simmer uncovered for 20 minutes, skimming often. Strain and cool.

STOCK, WHITE VEAL

Proceed as for brown stock, using only veal bones, but do not brown the bones and vegetables, and omit the tomato purée/paste. Blanch (see separate entry) the bones, then continue as for brown stock.

Core the tomatoes and mark a small cross at the **TOMATOES**
opposite end with the tip of a knife. Pour boiling **TO PEEL, SEED AND**
water over the tomatoes and leave for 10 seconds **CHOP**
or until the skin starts to peel at the cross. Drain
the tomatoes and peel them. Halve them crosswise,
squeeze them to remove the seeds, then chop
them. The seeds can be sieved to extract the juice.

Trussing encloses any stuffing and keeps a bird in **TRUSSING A BIRD**
shape so it cooks evenly. Remove the wishbone to
make carving easier: lift the neck skin and, with a
small sharp knife, outline the wishbone and cut it
free from the breastbone.

Set the bird breast up and push the legs back
and down so the legs are sticking straight up in the
air. Insert the trussing needle through one leg at the
joint, then out through the other leg joint. Turn the
bird over on to its other breast and push the needle
through both sections of one wing and then into
the neck skin, under the backbone of the bird,
and out the other side. Now catch the second
wing in the same way as the first. Pull the ends of
the string from the leg and wing firmly together and
tie securely.

Re-thread the trussing needle and turn the bird
breast side up. Tuck the tail into the cavity of the
bird. Insert the needle into the end of the drum-
stick, make a stitch through the skin, which should
be overlapping to cover the cavity, and then push
the needle through the end of the other drum-
stick. Turn the bird over and push the needle
through the tail. Tie the string ends together.

For ingredient measurements, see individual **VANILLA CUSTARD**
recipes. Scald the milk or milk and cream with **SAUCE**
the vanilla bean, splitting it to extract the seeds for
more flavour. Cover and leave to infuse for 10–15
minutes. Beat the egg yolks with the sugar until

thick and pale. Stir in the hot milk and return the mixture to the pan. Heat gently, stirring with a wooden spoon, until the custard thickens enough to leave a clear trail when you draw your finger across the back of a spoon (Note: do not boil or overcook the custard or it will curdle.) At once remove the custard from the heat and strain it into a bowl. The vanilla bean can be rinsed to use again.

Custard sauce can easily be flavoured. For coffee flavour, infuse the milk with coarsely ground coffee beans in place of the vanilla bean, straining the milk before mixing it with the egg yolk and sugar mixture. Or, you can add melted semi-sweet chocolate after the custard sauce has thickened and been removed from the heat.

VINAIGRETTE DRESSING

Vinaigrette dressing can be made with neutral vegetable oil, olive oil or nut oil. In France, red wine vinegar is most often used, but sometimes lemon juice is substituted (using roughly half of the quantity called for in vinegar). Other vinegars such as white wine, sherry, balsamic or fruit also make delicious vinaigrette dressings. Flavourings such as chopped onion, shallot, garlic or fresh herbs should be added to the dressing just before using. For measurements and specification of ingredients, see individual recipes. In a small bowl whisk the vinegar with the salt, pepper and any other seasonings (such as Dijon mustard) until the salt dissolves. Gradually add the oil, whisking constantly so that the dressing emulsifies and thickens slightly. Vinaigrette can be made ahead and kept for several days at room temperature; it will separate but will re-emulsify when whisked.

WATER BATH

Water baths are used both for cooking and for keeping food warm. Water diffuses direct heat and ensures food keeps moist and not too hot.

To cook in a water bath, bring a deep roasting

pan of water to the boil and set the mould or pan of food in it; the water should come at least halfway up the sides of the mould. Bring the water back to the boil and transfer to an oven heated to 375°F/ 190°C/ No 5 or continue cooking on top of the stove, according to the recipe. Count the cooking time from the moment the water comes to the boil.

To keep foods hot in a water bath: set the mould or pan in a roasting pan of hot but not boiling water and leave over very low heat. The water should not boil.

WHITE VEAL STOCK

See Stock, white veal

WILD MUSHROOMS
TO CLEAN

All fresh wild mushrooms need the same preparation. Pick them over to remove twigs and grass then lightly trim the stems. Shake and gently brush to remove any earth; morels are the most gritty, so brush each one well, splitting the stem to remove any soil inside. Rinse with cold water, but never soak fresh mushrooms as they quickly soften to a pulp.

Soak dried mushrooms in warm water for 1–2 hours until fairly soft. Morels may need rinsing again, but liquid from other mushrooms adds flavour to a soup or sauce. The flavour of both fresh and dried mushrooms varies very much in strength, but 2 lb/ 1 kg of fresh mushrooms is the approximate equivalent of 3 ¼ oz/ 100 g of dried mushrooms.

INDEX TO THE RECIPES

✣